Presented to:

_____

Presented by:

_____

Date:

_____

The wings of prayer carry high and far.

Project developed by Bordon Books, Tulsa, Oklahoma
Concept: Dave Bordon and Tom Winters
Project Writing: Andora Henson, Noelle Roso, Alison Simpson, Deborah Webb in association with SnapdragonGroup[SM] Editorial Services

FaithWords
Hachette Book Group USA
1271 Avenue of the Americas
New York, NY 10020

Visit our Web site at www.faithwords.com.

Printed in the United States of America

First Edition: November 2006
10 9 8 7 6 5 4 3 2 1

The FaithWords name and logo are trademarks of Hachette Book Group USA.

ISBN=10: 0-446-57936-x
ISBN=13: 978-0-446-57936-0

Anytime
Prayers
FOR
Everyday
Teens

New York Boston Nashville

Contents

Prayers of Confession 193

Lifting My Voice to God When I Need Forgiveness

Prayers of Intercession 223

Lifting My Voice to God on Behalf of Others

Prayers for my friends and family:

Prayers for the world around me:

Introduction

God wants to know you—and He wants you to know Him. It's a relationship He has invested His heart in. Does that surprise you? It shouldn't. You are God's most beloved creation, made in His own image. It's natural that He would want to communicate with you, and prayer is the means He has chosen to do just that.

Unfortunately, many people are intimidated by the idea of prayer. God seems so big, so powerful. Why would He care about our puny lives? Why would He want to hear about our troubles or heed our cries for help? The answers to those questions are beyond the scope of our limited understanding, but whatever His reason, the Bible says He does—care, hear, and answer.

Anytime Prayers for Everyday Teens contains the prayers of young people just like you—teens who have ups and downs of every kind. It is our hope that as you pray along with them within the pages of this book, you will feel God's loving touch on your own life.

O Precious Father, as we bow
Before Thy throne today—
We count the many blessings
Thou hast shower'd upon our way.

Author Unknown

Prayers
of Praise and
Thanksgiving

Lifting My Voice to God
for Who He Is and What He
Has Done for Me

When I want to thank God for His blessings . . .

O my soul, bless GOD.
From head to toe, I'll bless his holy name!
O my soul, bless GOD,
don't forget a single blessing!
He forgives your sins—every one.
He heals your diseases—every one.
He redeems you from hell—saves your life!
He crowns you with love and mercy—a paradise crown.
He wraps you in goodness—beauty eternal.
He renews your youth—you're always young in his presence.
PSALM 103:1-5 MSG

❖

From the fullness of his grace we have all received
one blessing after another.
JOHN 1:16

❖

Blessed be the God and Father of our Lord Jesus Christ,
who has blessed us with every spiritual blessing in the
heavenly places in Christ.
EPHESIANS 1:3 NASB

. . . I will pray.

Heavenly Father,

I want to thank You for the many blessings You have given me. The closer I get to You, the more I know that You are blessing me even when it does not feel like it. Thank You for showing me that blessings are more than possessions. They also include those things that money can't buy.

Thank You for the blessing of an education, Lord, even for the education that comes from life and circumstances. Thank You for the opportunity to use my knowledge and talents for Your glory. Thank You for friends and family. Thank You for the ability to dream, to hope, to laugh, and to love. I thank You, God, for all Your goodness to me, and I ask that You help me to be a channel of that goodness and grace to others.

Thank You, Lord, for all the ways—the countless ways—You've blessed me. My heart is filled with love and gratitude for You. My desire is to walk with You all the days of my life, for You are my great and caring God.

Amen.

Reflect upon your present blessings of which every man has many; not on your past misfortunes of which all men have some.

Charles Dickens

When I want to thank God for His creative genius . . .

In the beginning God created the heavens and the earth.
GENESIS 1:1 NKJV

❖

He merely spoke, and the heavens were formed, and all the galaxies of stars. He made the oceans, pouring them into his vast reservoirs. Let everyone in all the world—men, women, and children—fear the Lord and stand in awe of him.
PSALM 33:6-8 TLB

❖

You water the mountains from above.
The earth is full of the things you made.
You make the grass for cattle
and vegetables for the people.
PSALM 104:13-14 NCV

❖

Look up into the heavens. Who created all the stars?
He brings them out one after another, calling each by
its name. And he counts them to see that none
are lost or have strayed away.
ISAIAH 40:26 NLT

. . . I will pray.

Father God,

You are the Lord of splendor and glory. I look around at this world—Your beautiful masterpiece—and I'm amazed by what a remarkable Decorator You are. Infinite shades of blue, green, red—every color imaginable grace the landscape above, below, and around me. My senses feast on the majestic mountain scapes and the intricate flower blossoms. You are so much more than worthy of my praise.

Father, Your world is teeming with life—bright yellow butterflies, big, lazy hound dogs, amazingly beautiful flowers. Those who listen can hear the noisy serenading of crickets in the summer and the soothing music of a quickly flowing river. You, Lord, have decorated Your world with the touch of a true Master. Rugged trunks support boughs of delicate leaves as white, billowy clouds dance above our heads.

Thank You for creating this world for me to enjoy. I revel in Your creative genius. It is my privilege to live here in Your gallery, enjoying all of this. And then, I remember that I, too, am Your creation. The wonder of that leaves me speechless.

Amen.

Creativity is the basic attribute of God,
identical with his uniqueness.

Hermann Cohen

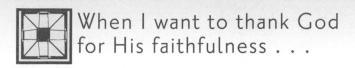# When I want to thank God for His faithfulness . . .

All the paths of the Lord are steadfast love and faithfulness,
for those who keep his covenant and his testimonies.
Psalm 25:10 RSV

❖

Even when we are too weak to have any faith left, [Christ]
remains faithful to us and will help us, for he cannot disown
us who are part of himself, and he will always carry out his
promises to us.
2 Timothy 2:13 TLB

❖

I face your Temple as I worship, giving thanks to you for all
your lovingkindness and your faithfulness, for your promises
are backed by all the honor of your name.
Psalm 138:2 TLB

❖

Your love, O Lord, reaches to the heavens,
Your faithfulness to the skies.
Psalm 36:5

. . . I will pray.

Heavenly Father,

Thank You for Your faithfulness that never fails. When I fall, You pick me up; when I am lost, You find me. When I don't know what to say, Your Holy Spirit speaks for me. When I become entangled in negative thoughts and behaviors, You set me free. I cannot thank You enough for the blessing of always knowing You are with me—in good times and bad times and at all times.

Seeing You work in my life, knowing that I can count on You makes me want to be better, more faithful myself. Thank You for being a Friend who sticks closer than a brother. Thank You for never leaving me nor forsaking me, for allowing me to be me but loving me enough to show me where I need to change.

There is very little that I can depend on in this world, Lord. But I know I can depend on You. That gives me courage to face my circumstances, my future, and even myself. Because You are faithful, I can be fearless in the world around me.

Amen.

God's investment in us is so great
he could not possibly abandon us.

Erwin W. Lutzer

When I want to thank God for His forgiveness . . .

If You, LORD, should mark iniquities,
O Lord, who could stand?
But there is forgiveness with You.
PSALM 130:3-4 NASB

❖

All the prophets testify about him that everyone who believes
in him receives forgiveness of sins through his name.
ACTS 10:43

❖

If we confess our sins, He is faithful and just to forgive us our
sins and to cleanse us from all unrighteousness.
1 JOHN 1:9 NKJV

❖

Oh, what joy for those
whose rebellion is forgiven,
whose sin is put out of sight!
Yes, what joy for those
whose record the LORD has cleared of sin,
whose lives are lived in complete honesty!
PSALM 32:1-2 NLT

. . . I will pray.

Father God,

I really messed up this time. I knew I was pushing the limits. I just wanted to fit in and have some fun. Still, I knew that there was a possibility—okay, a probability—that I would step out of Your will for me; and I went anyway. It was hard for me to come to You because there is no way to undo what I have done. Nevertheless, You are such an awesome God. When I asked for forgiveness You gave it.

You ran to me and met me on the road back to You, like the loving Father in the story of the prodigal son. I do not fully understand Your patience and Your grace, but I thank You for it. Thank You for using forgiveness to teach me rather than to shame me. Thank You for forgiveness that restores me to a right relationship with You and that makes me want to be better. Thank You for forgiveness that is complete as soon as I ask for and accept it. Thank You, Father God, for Your forgiveness. Everything in me is grateful.

Amen.

When God pardons, he consigns the offense
to everlasting forgetfulness.

Merv Rosell

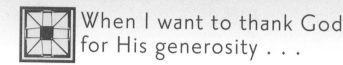

When I want to thank God for His generosity . . .

Generous to a fault,
you [God] lavish your favor on all creatures.
PSALM 145:16 MSG

❖

All sunshine and sovereign is GOD,
generous in gifts and glory.
He doesn't scrimp with his traveling companions.
PSALM 84:11 MSG

❖

Splendor and beauty mark his craft;
His generosity never gives out.
His miracles are his memorial.
This GOD *of Grace, this* GOD *of Love.*
PSALM 111:3-4 MSG

❖

To him who is able to do immeasurably more than all we ask
or imagine, according to his power that is at work within us,
to him be glory in the church.
EPHESIANS 3:20-21

. . . I will pray.

Lord God,

I know that there are others who are needier than I am. Sometimes, I feel like I shouldn't come to You with too many problems or requests. Still, when I do come, You always make me feel so good about it, like You really care and enjoy pouring out Your love and blessings on me. You are more generous than anyone I've ever known.

That shouldn't surprise me really. After all, I've read in the Bible that You know even the number of hairs on my head. You created me and gave me everything that I have in my life—my family, my friends, my unique personality and temperament. I guess that's why You are so generous with me—because I belong to You.

Thank You for not only knowing and meeting my needs but for going beyond what I ask or imagine. I thank You, God, for Your generosity and the love I feel when I see You caring for me. It makes me want to share more of me with others and more of You with everyone. You fill my heart to overflowing.

Amen.

Accustom yourself to the wonderful thought that God loves you with a tenderness, a generosity, and an intimacy that surpasses all your dreams.

Abbe Henri de Tourville

When I want to thank God
for His goodness . . .

I am still confident of this:
I will see the goodness of the LORD
in the land of the living.
PSALM 27:13

The LORD is good to all,
And His mercies are over all His works.
PSALM 145:9 NASB

How great is your goodness,
which you have stored up for those who fear you,
which you bestow in the sight of men
on those who take refuge in you.
PSALM 31:19

In his goodness he chose to make us his own children
by giving us his true word. And we, out of all creation,
became his choice possession.
JAMES 1:18 NLT

. . . I will pray.

Heavenly Father,

There are times when the weight of the world seems to be on my shoulders. I watch the news, and it fills me with sadness. Why are people so cruel to each other? Sometimes it seems like there is no goodness in any of us. If only everyone could recognize Your goodness—the wonderful way You reach out to all of us, loving and caring for us. Open their eyes, Lord, so that they can see what is right in front of them.

Until then, I will be here praising and acknowledging Your goodness in my life. I will celebrate Your love and compassion. I will surround myself with the light rather than the darkness. I will wrap myself in the joy You give rather than the sorrow the world settles for.

This is an extraordinary day, Lord, especially this very moment when I can feel Your goodness in everything. I just want so much to stop and say, Thank You. It makes me want to share Your goodness with everyone I meet.

Amen.

The Lord's goodness surrounds us at every moment. I walk through it almost with difficulty, as through thick grass and flowers.

R. W. Barbour

When I want to thank God for His gifts . . .

Just as we have many members in one body and all the members do not have the same function, so we, who are many, are one body in Christ, and individually members one of another. Since we have gifts that differ according to the grace given to us, each of us is to exercise them accordingly.

ROMANS 12:4-6 NASB

*When he ascended on high,
he led captives in his train
and gave gifts to men.*

EPHESIANS 4:8

Concerning spiritual gifts . . . I do not want you to be uninformed. . . . There are varieties of gifts, but the same Spirit; and there are varieties of services, but the same Lord; and there are varieties of activities, but it is the same God who activates all of them in everyone. To each is given the manifestation of the Spirit for the common good.

1 CORINTHIANS 12:1, 4-7 NRSV

. . . I will pray.

Dear God,

Thank You for showing me that the gifts You've placed in my life aren't for me at all—they are intended to bring glory to You. Now that I know the truth, I don't hold back. I work to identify and develop every single gift, and when someone asks me about them, I have a chance to tell that person about You.

Thank You, Lord, for all the special gifts and abilities You've given me. I don't deserve anything from You, and yet, You have been so generous. And seeing my gifts keeps me from focusing on my weaknesses.

Every time I use my gift, Lord, I pray that it would be pleasing to You, that it would bring joy to Your heart, and that it would show the world that You are much more than a God way up in heaven who doesn't care about us or what we're doing. And in return, I promise to keep on making the most of everything I've been given.

Amen.

Your talent is God's gift to you. What you do with it is your gift back to God.

Leo Buscaglia

When I want to thank God for His grace . . .

The amazing grace of the Master, Jesus Christ,
the extravagant love of God, the intimate friendship of
the Holy Spirit, be with all of you.
2 CORINTHIANS 13:14 MSG

❖

From his fullness we have all received, grace upon grace.
The law indeed was given through Moses;
grace and truth came through Jesus Christ.
JOHN 1:16-17 NRSV

❖

Even though on the outside it often looks like things
are falling apart on us, on the inside, where God is making
new life, not a day goes by without his unfolding grace.
2 CORINTHIANS 4:16 MSG

❖

If your life honors the name of Jesus, he will honor you. Grace
is behind and through all of this, our God giving himself
freely, the Master, Jesus Christ, giving himself freely.
2 THESSALONIANS 1:12 MSG

. . . I will pray.

Father God,

This grace business is a new concept for me. I don't know much about it—except that I have no right to ask for anything from You, but because of grace, I can. That's pretty amazing, and I want to thank You for it.

Some people say grace is kindness or compassion. Others say it is unearned favor and it can't be repaid. I don't know about all that. But what I do know is that You're awesome and perfect and mighty. I'm just a teenager, a nobody who messes up pretty much all the time—and yet, You love me, You want to spend time with me, You want to erase my sins and help me be a better person. If that's grace, then it's pretty wonderful and thank You for it.

I don't know of anything I could do to pay You back for such a big gift—maybe that's what the whole "unearned" part is all about. I just know that I'm grateful and I'll try as hard as I can not to waste it or forget it. I'll always treat with respect and honor the relationship we have because of grace.

Amen.

Grace comes into the soul, as the morning sun into the world; first a dawning, then a light; and at last the sun in his full and excellent brightness.

Thomas Adams

When I want to thank God for His joy . . .

We are praying . . . that you will be filled with his mighty, glorious strength so that you can keep going no matter what happens—always full of the joy of the Lord.
COLOSSIANS 1:11 TLB

❖

You will make known to me the path of life;
In Your presence is fullness of joy.
PSALM 16:11 NASB

❖

Shout for joy to the LORD, all the earth.
Worship the LORD with gladness;
come before him with joyful songs.
PSALM 100:1-2

❖

[The Lord says] The joy of the LORD will fill you to overflowing. You will glory in the Holy One of Israel.
ISAIAH 41:16 NLT

❖

Be full of joy in the Lord always.
I will say again, be full of joy.
PHILIPPIANS 4:4 NCV

. . . I will pray.

Dear Heavenly Father,

Since I met You something is different. It has always been easy for me to feel happy when I pass a test or make a new friend or something like that. But now, I don't know how to explain it—even when things are upsetting or uncomfortable, or even all messed up, I have this joyful feeling deep down inside. It's like someone stuck a message on my heart that says, "Smile, God loves you."

Thank You, God, for this joy—it must be from You, because on the outside I have the same life as I've always had—the same family, the same school, the same friends. The change is all on the inside. It's like a happy little secret inside me that tells me things are different now. I have You and that's something I can always be happy about.

Thank You, Lord, for making it possible for me to feel joyful even when things aren't so good. Show me how to share this joy with others. I know they need it and need You as much as I ever did.

Amen.

I have no understanding of a long-faced Christian.
If God is anything, he must be joy.

Joe E. Brown

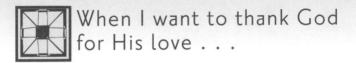# When I want to thank God for His love . . .

Give thanks to the LORD, for he is good;
his love endures forever.
PSALM 118:29

❖

God's love will continue forever.
PSALM 52:1 NCV

❖

This is what real love is: It is not our love for God;
it is God's love for us in sending his Son to be
the way to take away our sins.
1 JOHN 4:10 NCV

❖

[Jesus said] God so loved the world that he gave his one
and only Son, that whoever believes in him shall not perish
but have eternal life.
JOHN 3:16

❖

We love Him because He first loved us.
1 JOHN 4:19 NKJV

. . . I will pray.

Father God,

I don't know much about love, except the basic stuff—my family loves me and I love them. My friends love me and I love them back. But I'm not sure why You would love me—You being so great and mighty and perfect and all. I don't really get why, but I sure am glad You do.

Your love has changed my whole life. I don't feel like a loser anymore—but like I'm someone special. That's pretty great. I know that Jesus vouched for me, took care of all my mistakes, and introduced me to You. And I know that meant giving up His own life. I've never had a friend like Him before. Thank You, Lord, for sending Him to come and rescue me.

I would be nowhere and have nothing without You, Father. No future. No plans. No happiness. But Your love has changed all that. How will I ever be able to thank You enough? I just pray that I can love You back with all my heart and that I can share Your love with everyone I meet.

Amen.

God does not love us because we are valuable.
We are valuable because God loves us.

Archbishop Fulton J. Sheen

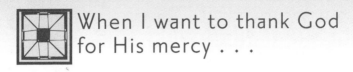

When I want to thank God for His mercy . . .

Generous in love—God, give grace!
Huge in mercy—wipe out my bad record.
PSALM 51:1 MSG

❖

All those who know your mercy, Lord, will count on you for
help. For you have never yet forsaken those who trust in you.
PSALM 9:10 TLB

❖

I will always trust in you and in your mercy and
shall rejoice in your salvation. I will sing to the Lord
because he has blessed me so richly.
PSALM 13:5-6 TLB

❖

God is sheer mercy and grace;
not easily angered, he's rich in love.
PSALM 103:8 MSG

❖

You can't whitewash Your sins and get by with it;
You find mercy by admitting and leaving them.
PROVERBS 28:13 MSG

. . . I will pray.

Father God,

"No mercy." I saw that on somebody's T-shirt one day. I felt bad about it. Did that person mean that he had no intention of giving mercy to anyone else, or did he mean that he never got any mercy in his life? He might have thought it was just an interesting shirt, but I wish I'd told him about You.

If anyone could say "No mercy," it's You. You don't need mercy from anyone and You have no need to offer it to anyone else either—except that You do. I read in the Bible—I think it was the book of Psalms—that You have heard my cry for mercy and accepted my prayer. That's about the greatest thing I've ever heard about.

Thank You, Lord, for having mercy on me, for reaching out to me and not just throwing me away because I wasn't perfect. Thanks for finding a way to buy me back and making something good and special with my life. My heart is full of gratitude and praise.

Amen.

Our faults are like a grain of sand beside the
great mountain of the mercies of God.

Saint Jean Baptiste Marie Vianney

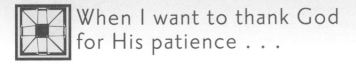

When I want to thank God for His patience . . .

The fruit of the Spirit is . . . patience.
GALATIANS 5:22 NASB

❖

*The Lord is not slow about His promise, as some count
slowness, but is patient toward you, not wishing for any to
perish but for all to come to repentance.*
2 PETER 3:9 NASB

❖

*God had mercy on me, so that Christ Jesus could use me
as a prime example of his great patience with even
the worst sinners.*
1 TIMOTHY 1:16 NLT

❖

*With patience you can convince a ruler,
and a gentle word can get through to the hard-headed.*
PROVERBS 25:15 NCV

❖

The patient in spirit is better than the proud in spirit.
ECCLESIASTES 7:8 RSV

. . . I will pray.

Heavenly Father,

You know that saying: "Been there, done that, bought the T-shirt"? Well, that is how I feel lately. I feel as if I am making the same mistakes over and over again, tripping up and falling for the same old temptations.

I don't know how You do it—forgiving me and then forgiving me again and then forgiving again! I'd go crazy if I had to deal with me. After a while, I'd just say, "Forget about it. This person is hopeless." But You never do that. Your patience is so amazing. Each time I come to You, You say, "I forgive you." You give me a first start, a second start, a third start . . . and You never give up on me or send me away. You treat me with kindness and love no matter what.

You probably already know how grateful I am for Your love and patience, but I want to tell You anyway. I'm sorry for those times that I push Your patience to the extreme. Help me to respond to Your patient love by being more patient with myself and others.

Amen.

God's love for poor sinners is very wonderful,
but God's patience with ill-natured saints is
a deeper mystery.

Henry Drummond

When I want to thank God for His peace . . .

Following after the Holy Spirit leads to life and peace.
ROMANS 8:6 TLB

❖

Let the peace of heart which comes from Christ be always present in your hearts and lives, for this is your responsibility and privilege as members of his body.
COLOSSIANS 3:15 TLB

❖

The punishment that brought us peace was upon him.
ISAIAH 53:5

❖

[Jesus said] I am leaving you with a gift—peace of mind and heart! And the peace I give isn't fragile like the peace the world gives. So don't be troubled or afraid.
JOHN 14:27 TLB

❖

While they were still talking about this, Jesus himself stood among them and said to them, "Peace be with you."
LUKE 24:36

. . . I will pray.

Heavenly Father,

Not more than a few minutes ago, I felt like there was a tornado inside my head. Everything was swirling, spinning, out of control. Between school, home, my job, and all the other stuff that's going on in my life, I felt like one big anxious ball. I needed Your peace, Lord, and sure enough—as soon as I asked, it was there. The only thing I don't understand is why it took me so long to ask.

Thank You, Lord, for Your peace. It's the most incredible thing I've ever experienced—like a beautiful, placid lake right in the middle of a hurricane. I know it's a miracle. I also know that the chaos in my head is my own fault. I should be sending those stressful thoughts on to You and being more responsible about leaving time for my mind to unwind and settle down. With Your help, Lord, I'll try to do better from now on.

Remind me to ask You each morning when I get up and every night before I go to bed for Your peace to flood my mind. And, Lord, You know that I'm grateful. I thank You with all my heart.

Amen.

God is a tranquil being and abides in a tranquil eternity. So must your spirit become a tranquil and clear little pool, wherein the serene light of God can be mirrored.

Gerhard Tersteegen

When I want to thank God for His presence . . .

Wonderful times of refreshment will come from
the presence of the Lord.
ACTS 3:20 NLT

❖

I was filled with delight day after day,
rejoicing always in his presence.
PROVERBS 8:30

❖

God has made you his friends again. He did this through
Christ's death in the body so that he might bring you into
God's presence as people who are holy.
COLOSSIANS 1:22 NCV

❖

Be still in the presence of the LORD,
and wait patiently for him to act.
PSALM 37:7 NLT

❖

Let us come before His presence with thanksgiving.
PSALM 95:2 NKJV

. . . I will pray.

Father God,

I never thought that someone like You would want to hang out with someone like me. How amazing is that! You could spend Your time admiring Your incredible universe or with people a lot more important and spiritual than I am, but here You are. I can feel You inside, making me feel peaceful and happy and complete.

Thank You, Lord, for wanting to be with me. Your love is a mystery I can never solve. It's way too high and wonderful for my simple mind. Even more of a miracle is that Your love causes You to reach out to me and even send Your Holy Spirit to live right inside me. I read in the Bible that You were standing at the door of my heart, knocking, and if I opened the door and invited You in, You would stay there forever. I did open the door and You kept Your promise too. Now I feel You with me, and I'm filled with gratitude.

Give me the words, Lord, to tell my friends and family that they can invite You into their lives just like I did. Something this wonderful has to be shared.

Amen.

As his child, you are entitled to his kingdom,
the warmth, the peace, and the
power of his presence.

Author Unknown

When I want to thank God for His protection . . .

He shall give His angels charge over you,
To keep you in all your ways.
PSALM 91:11 NKJV

❖

The LORD loves the just
and will not forsake his faithful ones.
They will be protected forever.
PSALM 37:28

❖

Happy are those who trust him for protection.
PSALM 2:12 NCV

❖

Let all who take refuge in you be glad;
let them ever sing for joy.
Spread your protection over them,
that those who love your name may rejoice in you.
PSALM 5:11

❖

The LORD keeps you from all evil and preserves your life.
The LORD keeps watch over you as you come and go,
both now and forever.
PSALM 121:7-8 NLT

. . . I will pray.

Father God,

I read in the Bible that You've sent Your angels to watch over me and protect me in all my ways. They must be busy creatures because I somehow always seem to be finding dangers to involve myself in. I don't mean to, but I have a habit of acting before I think and listening too much to my friends.

I promise to be more responsible about that, Lord. I know I can't avoid trouble altogether—no one can—but I can do a better job of listening to Your voice and making more thoughtful choices.

Right now, though, I just want to thank You, Lord, for watching over me—even when I've been foolish, flirted with disaster, and pushed the boundaries. I know when I do those things, it's hurtful to You and to those who love me, and it jeopardizes all Your plans for my life.

You are such a caring God, faithful even when I'm not. I don't deserve Your love and protection, but You give it right along with Your forgiveness. Thanks, Lord, for everything.

Amen.

We sleep in peace in the arms of God.
François de Salignac de La Mothe-Fénelon

When I want to thank God for His provision . . .

My God shall supply all your need according to his riches in glory by Christ Jesus.
PHILIPPIANS 4:19 KJV

[Jesus said] Don't worry about food—what to eat and drink; don't worry at all that God will provide it for you. All mankind scratches for its daily bread, but your heavenly Father knows your needs. He will always give you all you need from day to day if you will make the Kingdom of God your primary concern.
LUKE 12:29-31 TLB

His divine power has given us everything needed for life and godliness, through the knowledge of him who called us by his own glory and goodness.
2 PETER 1:3 NRSV

I will provide for their needs before they ask, and I will help them while they are still asking for help.
ISAIAH 65:24 NCV

. . . I will pray.

Dear Father,

Asking for help is hard for me. I have this fear that people will make fun of me. That's why it's so nice that I can come to You. You never make me feel bad for asking, and You always provide for me—no matter if it's a spiritual need or a physical or emotional one.

I want to give You all the thanks You deserve for that. I don't know what I'd do if You weren't here to help me anymore. You've been tugging at my heart, though, haven't You? I've felt it. And I think You're trying to help me give up my fear and start to trust people more, especially those people who go out of their way to help teens like me.

So I guess this time I'm asking You for a provision of another kind. Provide me with courage, Lord, and wisdom, and lead me to someone who can help with the things I need. You've been so good to me that it makes me hope that others will be too.

Thank You, Lord, for all Your provisions. You've never turned me away or left me standing there looking stupid with empty hands. Somehow, You've always provided. I'm very grateful. Now help me trust You more as I take the next step.

Amen.

God is absolutely unlimited in His ability and His resources. And He is unlimited in His desire to pour out those resources upon us.

Gloria Copeland

When I want to thank God for His salvation . . .

[Peter said] Jesus is the only One who can save people. His name is the only power in the world that has been given to save people. We must be saved through him.

ACTS 4:12 NCV

❖

If you confess with your mouth the Lord Jesus and believe in your heart that God has raised Him from the dead, you will be saved.

ROMANS 10:9 NKJV

❖

I am not ashamed of the gospel: it is the power of God for salvation to every one who has faith.

ROMANS 1:16 RSV

❖

He saved us—not because we were good enough to be saved, but because of his kindness and pity—by washing away our sins and giving us the new joy of the indwelling Holy Spirit.

TITUS 3:5 TLB

. . . I will pray.

Heavenly Father,

I thought that because I was a normal person, a good person even, that I did not need You. I thought that being obedient, getting good grades, and not making trouble meant that I was bound for heaven. I thought going to church on Sunday made all the difference, and if I put in my time once a week I was safe.

Thank You for sending someone into my life who told me the Truth—someone who had felt the same way I did about being a good kid and being okay without You. You sent someone to clear things up and show me the way to You, God, and I thank You.

I'm so grateful for the gift of salvation that I can never earn and for Your Son, Jesus, who covered up my mistakes with His perfect blood. Thank You for showing me that being "good" is not "good enough," but His goodness is all I will ever need.

Please send someone into my life whom I can share this gift with—someone I can lead to You.

Amen.

Salvation is a gift you can ask for.

Author Unknown

When I want to thank God for His wisdom . . .

God's wisdom is deep, and his power is great.
JOB 9:4 NCV

❖

Wisdom will make your life pleasant
and will bring you peace.
As a tree produces fruit, wisdom gives life to those who use it,
and everyone who uses it will be happy.
PROVERBS 3:17-18 NCV

❖

God's words will always prove true and right,
no matter who questions them.
ROMANS 3:4 TLB

❖

I pray for you constantly, asking God, the glorious Father
of our Lord Jesus Christ, to give you wisdom to see clearly
and really understand who Christ is and
all that he has done for you.
EPHESIANS 1:16-17 TLB

. . . I will pray.

Dear Lord,

I always wondered about King Solomon in the Bible. He could have asked for anything from You—after all, You created the heavens and the earth—but he chose wisdom. For a while, I thought he must have been crazy or something. But now I'm starting to see how he was thinking.

Money, possessions, popularity, and even knowledge are limited. They reach only certain aspects of life—and they're tough to hold on to, changing with every new circumstance in a person's life. But wisdom—that's different.

Wisdom can help me make good choices every time. It can help me see below the surface of situations and avoid major mistakes that cause setbacks in my life. Things like what to do after I get out of school, what job to choose, whom to marry, where to live—those are all decisions that can change my life for good or bad, and the key to getting them right is wisdom.

Thank You, Lord, for giving me the wisdom I need for each decision—big and small—in my life.

Amen.

Most of us go through life praying a little, planning a little, . . . hoping but never being quite certain of anything, and always secretly afraid that we will miss the way. . . . There is a better way. It is to repudiate our own wisdom and take instead the infinite wisdom of God.

A. W. Tozer

Were half the breath that's vainly spent,
To heaven in supplication sent,
Our cheerful song would oftener be,
"Hear what the Lord has done for me."

Garnet Rolling

Prayers of Supplication

Lifting My Voice to God
When I Need Help

When I need to feel God's acceptance . . .

[Jesus said] The one who comes to Me
I will certainly not cast out.
JOHN 6:37 NASB

❖

Christ accepted you, so you should accept each other,
which will bring glory to God.
ROMANS 15:7 NCV

❖

"Return to me," declares the LORD Almighty,
"and I will return to you," says the LORD Almighty.
ZECHARIAH 1:3

❖

The God and Father of our Lord Jesus Christ . . .
made us accepted in the Beloved.
EPHESIANS 1:3, 6 NKJV

❖

Peter began to speak: "I now realize how true it is that God
does not show favoritism but accepts men from every nation
who fear him and do what is right."
ACTS 10:34-35

. . . I will pray.

Heavenly Father,

Some people have it made. Everybody wants to be their friend. They never have to worry about being accepted—ever. They wear the right clothes, say the right things, live in the right part of town. We both know I'm not one of the "cool" kids.

I try not to think about it, Lord—just kind of pretend I don't care. But it hurts not to have friends, to always feel like there's something wrong with me. I'd change if I could, but I have no idea where I would start to make myself fit in.

Thank You, Lord, for always being there for me. When things are tough at school and I come home feeling miserable and worthless, I know I can sneak up here to my room and talk to You for a few minutes and I'll feel better. You always make me feel that I'm okay—special even. Thank You for that. Help me to remember when I'm going through it at school that if You—the God who creates us all—loves and accepts me, then that's way better than being friends with a bunch of kids. Thank You for being my best Friend.

Amen.

Christianity is about acceptance, and if God accepts me as I am, then I had better do the same.

Hugh Montefiore

When I'm feeling anger . . .

Refrain from anger and turn from wrath;
do not fret—it leads only to evil.
PSALM 37:8

❖

Do not be quickly provoked in your spirit,
for anger resides in the lap of fools.
ECCLESIASTES 7:9

❖

Patience is better than strength.
Controlling your temper is better than capturing a city.
PROVERBS 16:32 NCV

❖

Put them all aside: anger, wrath, malice, slander, and abusive
speech from your mouth.
COLOSSIANS 3:8 NASB

❖

You must understand this, my beloved: let everyone be quick
to listen, slow to speak, slow to anger; for your anger does not
produce God's righteousness.
JAMES 1:19-20 NRSV

. . . I will pray.

Dear God,

I'm so mad right now that I don't even trust myself to talk to anyone—except You. I know I shouldn't let things get to me, but they always do. Somebody says or does something that irritates me, I strike back, and before I know it—well, You know . . . it's not pretty.

I've read in the Old Testament how You used to get angry with Your people when they rejected You and forgot about all You'd done for them. But then I've also read in the book of Psalms that You were merciful and forgiving to them. You could have crushed them, but instead You let go of Your anger and continued to love them.

I'm pretty glad that You don't just squash me when I've done something to hurt or wrong You, which happens just about every day. Instead, You keep loving and forgiving me, opening up Your arms to me every time. Teach me to let go of anger, to walk away from it, and become more like You.

Amen.

When angry, take a lesson from technology; always count down before blasting off.

Author Unknown

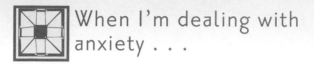

When I'm dealing with anxiety . . .

Anxiety weighs down the human heart,
but a good word cheers it up.
PROVERBS 12:25 NRSV

❖

When anxiety was great within me,
your consolation brought joy to my soul.
PSALM 94:19

❖

Cast all your anxiety on him because he cares for you.
1 PETER 5:7

❖

Be anxious for nothing, but in everything by prayer and
supplication, with thanksgiving, let your requests be made
known to God; and the peace of God, which surpasses all
understanding, will guard your hearts and minds through
Christ Jesus.
PHILIPPIANS 4:6-7 NKJV

❖

May God bless you richly and grant you increasing
freedom from all anxiety and fear.
1 PETER 1:2 TLB

. . . I will pray.

Father God,

It seems like I worry all the time—at home, at school, wherever I go. *Will people like me? What if I fail that big exam? What if I don't make the team?* One question at a time, it seems like those are logical questions—but when I look at them all together, I see that worry is taking over my life. It's stealing my fun, my happiness, and even my future.

I think I know what the problem is, Lord—I just haven't learned to trust You to watch over and manage those areas of my life that I can't watch over and manage myself. I want to control everything—make sure that all the bases are covered. And that leaves me with an anxious heart and impending disaster and You locked out, unable to help.

That can't be good for me. And that conclusion is confirmed by the rock in the pit of my stomach. So, I'm going to make a new beginning. By an act of my will, I'm going to turn over my life to You. It's just too hard being God of my own life. Thank You, Lord, for meeting me where I am.

Amen.

Man's world has become a nervous one,
encompassed by anxiety. God's world is other than
this; always balanced, calm, and in order.

Faith Baldwin

When I need answers . . .

Listen to this prayer of mine, GOD;
pay attention to what I'm asking.
Answer me—you're famous for your answers!
Do what's right for me.
PSALM 143:1 MSG

❖

I cry aloud to the LORD,
and he answers me from his holy hill.
PSALM 3:4 RSV

❖

Lord, hear my prayer! Listen to my plea!
Don't turn away from me in this time of my distress.
Bend down your ear and give me speedy answers.
PSALM 102:1-2 TLB

❖

Ask and it will be given to you; seek and you will find;
knock and the door will be opened to you.
For everyone who asks receives; he who seeks finds;
and to him who knocks, the door will be opened.
MATTHEW 7:7-8

. . . I will pray.

O Lord,

I have questions—lots of them. Questions about faith, about life, about eternity, about almost everything. My friends laugh at me and say, "Why do you have to make it so complicated?" I don't know why. It's just the way I'm built.

Lord, I know I'll never have all the answers here on earth. And I know all my questions don't exactly speak well of my faith. But I can't seem to be content to just blindly follow what others tell me about You and how things are supposed to be.

I want my faith in You to be rock solid. I want to know what I believe and why I believe it. I want to have such a knowing about Your character that I can stand strong and steady no matter what is going on around me. As I read my Bible and spend time with You in prayer, as I look around at the world You created and the way You relate to us here on earth, open my eyes to see the real You, the great You, the eternal You, the loving, gentle, wonderful You. When that happens, I feel like a lot of my questions will find their answers.

Amen.

God has never turned away the questions
of a sincere searcher.

Max L. Lucado

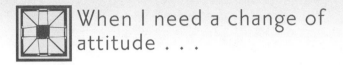 When I need a change of attitude . . .

Be made new in the attitude of your minds; and . . .
put on the new self, created to be like God in true
righteousness and holiness.
EPHESIANS 4:23-24

❖

A relaxed attitude lengthens life.
PROVERBS 14:30 NLT

❖

The Kingdom of God is not a matter of what we eat or
drink, but of living a life of goodness and peace and joy in the
Holy Spirit. If you serve Christ with this attitude, you will
please God.
ROMANS 14:17-18 NLT

❖

May God, who gives this patience and encouragement, help
you live in complete harmony with each other—each with the
attitude of Christ Jesus toward the other.
ROMANS 15:5 NLT

❖

The word of God is living and active. . . . It judges the
thoughts and attitudes of the heart.
HEBREWS 4:12

. . . I will pray.

Lord in Heaven,

I knew I was feeling a little cranky, but I didn't realize my attitude was that bad until people started telling me about it. All that did was make me mad and put me in a worse mood—that is, until I started wondering what You might think about the way I was acting.

Please forgive me, Lord, for behaving like a spoiled child, for taking my irritation out on other people, and for forgetting that You are there to help me deal with things. I guess I pretty much blew it all the way around. I want to be someone You can be proud of, someone who mirrors Your character.

As I place myself in Your care, Lord, I ask that You cleanse me inside and then encourage me. Give me hope that I can deal with life better tomorrow, be a better person tomorrow, show Your love to others more tomorrow. Thank You for yanking me up short and refusing to let me continue in my rebellious ways. You are a good and loving God.

Amen.

God . . . gives me the freedom to acknowledge
my negative attitudes . . . but not the freedom to act
them out because they are as destructive for me as
they are for the other person.

Rebecca Manley Pippert

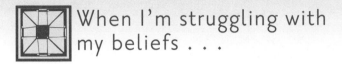# When I'm struggling with my beliefs . . .

If you are asked about your Christian hope,
always be ready to explain it.
1 PETER 3:15 NLT

❖

Study to shew thyself approved unto God, a workman that
needeth not to be ashamed, rightly dividing the word of truth.
2 TIMOTHY 2:15 KJV

❖

I pray for you constantly, asking God, the glorious Father of
our Lord Jesus Christ, to give you spiritual wisdom and
understanding, so that you might grow in your knowledge of
God.
EPHESIANS 1:16-17 NLT

❖

Faith comes from hearing the Good News, and people hear
the Good News when someone tells them about Christ.
ROMANS 10:17 NCV

❖

Teach me good discernment and knowledge,
For I believe in Your commandments.
PSALM 119:66 NASB

. . . I will pray.

Heavenly Father,

Today someone actually asked me if I believe in God—I knew the answer to that question, but all I could get out of my mouth was a weak little yes. I know You're real, but I don't know for sure why I believe it or how to explain it to others.

Help me to be strong and secure in my beliefs, Lord. I want to be able to answer intelligently when someone asks me what I believe. As I read the Bible, show me the Scriptures and principles my beliefs are based on. And help me to be a good student of my faith, increasing in knowledge and understanding about You and the wonderful plan You have in place to make us Your children.

I love You, Lord, and I want to be able to share You with others, to show others what a kind and good and accessible God You are. I want them to be able to believe in You just as I do. Show me how to become solidly established in my beliefs so that I can share them with others.

Amen.

What I believe about God is the most important thing about me.

A. W. Tozer

When I need help paying my bills . . .

God is able to make all grace (every favor and earthly
blessing) come to you in abundance, so that you may always
and under all circumstances and whatever the need be self-
sufficient [possessing enough to require no aid or support
and furnished in abundance for every good work
and charitable donation].

2 CORINTHIANS 9:8 AMP

❖

A slack hand causes poverty,
but the hand of the diligent makes rich.

PROVERBS 10:4 RSV

❖

This same God who takes care of me will supply all your
needs from his glorious riches, which have been given to us
in Christ Jesus.

PHILIPPIANS 4:19 NLT

❖

[Jesus said] Look at the birds of the air; they do not sow or
reap or store away in barns, and yet your heavenly Father
feeds them. Are you not much more valuable than they?

MATTHEW 6:26

. . . I will pray.

Heavenly Father,

I don't have that many bills, but I do have some, and I've tried to make sure that I could pay them all—but this month I can see that I'm not going to make it. Too many unexpected things came up, extra expenses I couldn't anticipate. Now, I need Your help to stretch and multiply what I have.

My situation must be small compared to some of the big financial problems people come to You with. Mine aren't a matter of life and death or even likely to leave me in financial ruin. But I believe You care about those things that are important to me even if they don't represent the end of the world as we know it.

Lord, show me what to do, how to manage this shortfall. If it means eating my pride and asking my parents for help, I'm willing to do that. If it means working extra hours at my job, I'm glad to do that also. I'll do my part if You'll just show me what my part is.

Thank You, Lord, for providing for all my needs.

Amen.

Cheer up: birds have bills too,
but they keep on singing.

Author Unknown

When I'm having trouble with my boyfriend . . .

Flee from sexual immorality. All other sins a man commits are outside his body, but he who sins sexually sins against his own body. Do you not know that your body is a temple of the Holy Spirit, who is in you, whom you have received from God? You are not your own; you were bought at a price. Therefore honor God with your body.

1 CORINTHIANS 6:18-20

Do not be yoked together with unbelievers. For what do righteousness and wickedness have in common? Or what fellowship can light have with darkness? What harmony is there between Christ and Belial? What does a believer have in common with an unbeliever? What agreement is there between the temple of God and idols? For we are the temple of the living God. As God has said: "I will live with them and walk among them, and I will be their God, and they will be my people."

2 CORINTHIANS 6:14-16

❖

You are not to keep company with anyone who claims to be a brother Christian but indulges in sexual sins.

1 CORINTHIANS 5:11 TLB

. . . I will pray.

Father God,

I am so angry! My boyfriend, who says he loves me with all his heart, is pressuring me to do things I don't feel right about doing. Many of my friends are going through the same thing. Most of them will do anything to please their boyfriends, and I might have, too, before I met You—but now I just want to make sure my life is pleasing to You.

Lord, even considering what I've just told You, I like my boyfriend. Sometimes I'm pretty sure I love him even. I ask You for the courage to let him know how I really feel. Then it will be his choice to decide if he wants to stay with me or move on to someone who will give him what he wants.

Thank You, Lord, for the assurance that even in this emotional situation, You will give me clear guidance. And no matter how it turns out, it will be for my best interests. Thanks for helping me make good choices for my life.

Amen.

> [Sex] is magnificent, an enormous privilege,
> but because of that the rules are
> tremendously strict and severe.
>
> Francis Devas

When I'm overwhelmed by cares . . .

The LORD lifts the burdens of those bent
beneath their loads.
PSALM 146:8 NLT

❖

I will relieve your shoulder of its burden;
I will free your hands from their heavy tasks.
PSALM 81:6 NLT

❖

When the cares of my heart are many,
thy consolations cheer my soul.
PSALM 94:19 RSV

❖

Cast your cares on the LORD
and he will sustain you.
PSALM 55:22

❖

Let him have all your worries and cares,
for he is always thinking about you and
watching everything that concerns you.
1 PETER 5:7 TLB

. . . I will pray.

God in Heaven,

I feel so alone. It seems as if the weight of the world is on my shoulders and no one even notices that I am crumbling under the load. My problems may be small potatoes to some people— when I look at them one by one, none of them seems huge— but to me it seems like I'm out in the ocean with the rip tide pulling me under and the waves crashing over my head.

Lord, I need help—Your help. I need someone bigger than I am, someone who can help me carry these burdens. I bow down at Your feet right now and offer them up to You. The last time I decided to do that, I tried to sort through them first: "I'm okay with this one. I can handle that one on my own." When my prayer was finished, I was as bad off as before.

This time will be different. I've learned to let go and let You bear my burdens. And this time I won't try to decide what to keep and what to give to You—it all has to go, every single care, big and small alike.

Thank You for being the one I can always count on.

Amen.

Tell God all that is in your heart, as one unloads one's heart, its pleasures and its pains, to a dear friend. Tell Him your troubles, that He may comfort you.

François de Salignac de La Mothe-Fénelon

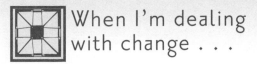 When I'm dealing
with change . . .

The LORD himself will go before you. He will be with you;
he will not leave you or forget you. Don't be afraid and
don't worry.

DEUTERONOMY 31:8 NCV

❖

[God said]
I'll go ahead of you,
clearing and paving the road.

ISAIAH 45:2 MSG

❖

I am the LORD, I change not.

MALACHI 3:6 KJV

❖

[The Lord says]
Do not remember the former things,
Nor consider the things of old.
Behold, I will do a new thing,
Now it shall spring forth;
Shall you not know it?
I will even make a road in the wilderness
And rivers in the desert.

ISAIAH 43:18-19 NKJV

. . . I will pray.

Lord God,

I can't explain why—but I hate change. It makes me feel confused and unsure of myself. You could call it disorienting. I depend on things being a certain way and then they aren't that way anymore.

Lord, I'm old enough to know that change is part of life. There's no way I can avoid it and refuse to deal with it. It's just going to always be there, in my face. You're the only one who can help me get from where I am to where I need to be.

I thought about asking You to give me a heads-up when change is in the wind, kind of a way for me to make a preemptive strike. Trouble is, I know You wouldn't go for that—that's not how You do things. So, Lord, I'm ready to let go of the tightfisted control I have over my life and let You take over. As I put my trust in You, I feel You will help me make whatever adjustments are needed as change comes blowing through.

Thank You, Lord, for looking past my human limitations and forcing me to face and overcome the obstacles in my life. I love You, and I'm glad to have You in my life.

Amen.

If we try to resist loss and change or to hold on to blessings and joy belonging to a past which must drop away from us, we postpone all the new blessings awaiting us on a higher level.

Hannah Hurnard

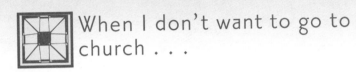

When I don't want to go to church . . .

Let us not neglect our church meetings, as some people do, but encourage and warn each other, especially now that the day of his coming back again is drawing near.

HEBREWS 10:25 TLB

❖

They were continually devoting themselves to
the apostles' teaching and to fellowship,
to the breaking of bread and to prayer.

ACTS 2:42 NASB

❖

On arriving there, they gathered the church together and
reported all that God had done through them.

ACTS 14:27

❖

Let the word of Christ dwell in you richly; teach and
admonish one another in all wisdom; and with gratitude in
your hearts sing psalms, hymns, and spiritual songs to God.

COLOSSIANS 3:16 NRSV

❖

Behold, how good and how pleasant it is
For brothers to dwell together in unity!

PSALM 133:1 NASB

. . . I will pray.

Lord God,

Can we talk? I really want to be a good person and do all of the right things, but I could sleep an extra three hours every Sunday morning if You would just let me know that it's okay to miss church. I don't see why it's such a big deal anyway. I see almost all the same people every Sunday, and half the time even the adults don't get along.

Sure, I admit that good things have happened to me there. Sometimes, the pastor will talk about a Scripture that I have been thinking about for a while. He'll explain it in a way that I never would have thought about on my own. And I can see where it's important for Christians to meet and pray together about stuff people have trouble handling on their own. I guess it's pretty important to be able to build friendships with other people who love You.

As good as that three extra hours of sleep sounds, Lord, I'm beginning to think that church is pretty important after all. Thank You, Lord, for helping me to answer my own question, and thank You for all the wonderful things my church adds to my life.

Amen.

Church-goers are like coals in a fire.
When they cling together, they keep the flame aglow;
when they separate, they die out.

Billy Graham

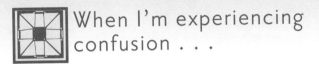# When I'm experiencing confusion . . .

God is not a God of confusion but of peace.

1 CORINTHIANS 14:33 NASB

❖

[David said]
You are my lamp, O LORD;
The LORD shall enlighten my darkness.

2 SAMUEL 22:29 NKJV

❖

Let him who walks in the dark,
who has no light,
trust in the name of the LORD
and rely on his God.

ISAIAH 50:10

❖

Lady Wisdom goes to town, stands in a prominent place,
and invites everyone within sound of her voice:
"Are you confused about life, don't know what's going on?
Come with me, oh come, have dinner with me!"

PROVERBS 9:3-4 MSG

. . . I will pray.

Heavenly Father,

I feel as if I am looking through a fun-house mirror. Everything seems distorted and unfamiliar. Just when I believe I'm starting to figure things out, something changes and I'm back on the blind side.

Lord, I'm no Bible scholar but I do know that confusion is not what You want for my life. You want me to walk clear and free, making right decisions and good choices for my life. You don't want me to walk around in the dark, stripped of my power and unable to fulfill the purpose for which You created me.

So, Father, I ask You to clear my head until I see things clearly. Speak to my heart in soft, gentle tones that I can focus on through the noise and discord. And I promise to be listening, following, taking hold of each word and letting You use it to lead me onto the paths of peace that lead to Your perfect will.

Thank You for turning me away from my inner fog and focusing my mind and heart on You. I know that confusion can't stay in the presence of the King of Peace.

Amen.

The greatest moments of your life are those when through all the confusion God got a message through to you plain and certain.

Bertha Munro

When I need courage . . .

It is impossible for God to lie. Therefore, we who have fled to him for refuge can take new courage, for we can hold on to his promise with confidence.
HEBREWS 6:18 NLT

❖

[The Lord said] Be bold and strong! Banish fear and doubt! For remember, the Lord your God is with you wherever you go.
JOSHUA 1:9 TLB

❖

Overwhelming victory is ours through Christ who loved us enough to die for us.
ROMANS 8:37 TLB

❖

*I am the LORD, your God,
who takes hold of your right hand
and says to you, Do not fear;
I will help you.*
ISAIAH 41:13

. . . I will pray.

Heavenly Father,

It's not that I don't know what to do. It's just that I'm having a little trouble psyching myself up to do it. I've never faced anything quite like this before.

I'm going to need help, Lord—a lot of help! I'm going to need to feel Your presence with me every single step of the way. I'm going to need peace. I'm going to need wisdom. And most of all, I'm going to need courage—the good, old-fashioned, supernatural kind.

You must have given David courage. How else could a young shepherd boy have stood up to that giant Goliath and cleaned his clock with nothing but a slingshot and a couple of smooth stones? And I'm thinking about others—Daniel, who had the courage to face lions; the three Hebrew teens who got themselves thrown into a fiery furnace and lived to tell about it. That's the kind of courage I need right now, because this thing I'm facing sure looks to me like a giant surrounded by lions standing in front of a fiery furnace. Thanks, Lord, for helping me face my fears and claim my victory.

Amen.

Courage is fear that has said its prayers.

Dorothy Bernard

When I'm concerned about
dating . . .

*Be careful how you live, not as fools but as those who are
wise. . . . Don't act thoughtlessly, but try to understand what
the Lord wants you to do.*
EPHESIANS 5:15, 17 NLT

❖

*Whatever you do, whether in word or deed,
do it all in the name of the Lord Jesus.*
COLOSSIANS 3:17

❖

Can two walk together, unless they are agreed?
AMOS 3:3 NKJV

❖

*Stay alert, be in prayer, so you don't enter the danger zone
without even knowing it. Don't be naïve.*
MARK 14:38 MSG

❖

*You are not the same as those who do not believe.
So do not join yourselves to them. . . . Light and darkness
cannot share together. . . . What can a believer have
together with a nonbeliever?*
2 CORINTHIANS 6:14-15 NCV

. . . I will pray.

Heavenly Father,

I love my life, running around having fun with my friends. Between school, church, my family, and my friends, something is always going on. There's really only one part of it that scares me a little. That's dating. How will I know whom to date—and when? Group dates? Couple dates? A friend of mine from church says she doesn't plan to date at all but to just pray and ask You to point out the one she should marry when the time is right. And scariest of all—what if no one wants to date me?

I'm looking to You for guidance, Lord. I know You will help me make the best choices at each point along the way. Help me to be wise about the people I say yes to and thoughtful about the things we do together. And I promise that I'll always listen to Your voice deep down inside me.

I know You are always with me, Lord—always pointing me in the right direction and always watching over me. Thank You for helping me take all this scary dating/relationship business and turn it into a positive adventure in my path to maturity.

Amen.

In His will is our peace.
Dante Alighieri

When I'm struggling with depression . . .

My soul melts from heaviness;
Strengthen me according to Your word.
PSALM 119:28 NKJV

❖

Come quickly, LORD, and answer me,
for my depression deepens.
Don't turn away from me, or I will die.
Let me hear of your unfailing love to me in the morning,
for I am trusting you.
PSALM 143:7-8 NLT

God, Who comforts and encourages and refreshes and cheers
the depressed and the sinking, comforted and encouraged
and refreshed and cheered us.
2 CORINTHIANS 7:6 AMP

❖

[God said to Noah] I have placed my rainbow in the clouds
as a sign of my promise until the end of time,
to you and to all the earth.
GENESIS 9:13 TLB

. . . I will pray.

Gracious God,

I've been having some gloomy days lately. I try to see each day as a new start, but that's not always easy to do. I live my life, go to school, hang out with friends, but sometimes I don't feel up to doing those things. In fact, I'm feeling pretty down right now. Can You lift me up?

I think of Noah, how You got him through that massive flood, and then came Your rainbow—Your promise of love and grace to everyone. And the people that Jesus healed—the blind, the sick, and even Lazarus, whom Jesus raised from the dead. Wow! You can do anything!

I remember as a child watching the rain stop, and the sun coming out, and looking up into the bright, warm sky to see a beautiful rainbow. I want to see this "rain" end and feel the warm brightness of love and promise and possibility. I'm already beginning to see through the gray skies and spot Your blessings in my life—the blessings of my family, friends, and what the future has in store for me.

Help me turn my eyes up to You and see Your rainbows. And thank You, God, for turning my gray skies to blue.

Amen.

It takes both the rain and the sunshine
to make a rainbow.

Author Unknown

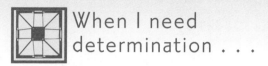

When I need determination . . .

The sluggard craves and gets nothing,
but the desires of the diligent are fully satisfied.
PROVERBS 13:4

❖

To this end we always pray for you, that our God may make
you worthy of his call, and may fulfil every good resolve and
work of faith by his power, so that the name of our Lord Jesus
may be glorified in you, and you in him, according to the
grace of our God and the Lord Jesus Christ.
2 THESSALONIANS 1:11-12 RSV

❖

Don't waver in resolve. Don't fear. Don't hesitate.
Don't panic. GOD, your God, is right there with you,
fighting with you.
DEUTERONOMY 20:3-4 MSG

❖

[David said] Strengthen your resolve and
do what must be done.
2 SAMUEL 2:7 MSG

. . . I will pray.

Almighty God,

I work a lot! I'm studying hard in school, going to soccer practice, helping out at church and in my youth group, and I've even got a job. But even with all that, there's something else I want to do. It's this big dream I've got. It's an aspiration that means a lot to me. I want it so badly! I know it won't just fall into my lap. I know I have to work hard if I want to make my big dream happen. So now I need to put my money where my mouth is. I need the determination to make my big dream a reality.

I know some people who think big dreams are silly. I think they need to open their eyes to what You can do with our lives. I'm inspired by so many others who had a dream and were determined to make it happen. I know it won't always be easy. Do I have what it takes to accomplish my dream? I believe I do, if I have You, Lord. Be my Guide. Be my Strength. Be my Determination, so that I have firm purpose to keep working and never give up.

Thank You for your loving guidance and constant strength. Amen.

The difference between the impossible and the possible lies in a man's determination.

Tommy Lasorda

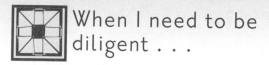

When I need to be diligent . . .

I am still not all I should be, but I am focusing all my
energies on this one thing: Forgetting the past and looking
forward to what lies ahead, I strain to reach the end of the
race and receive the prize for which God, through Christ
Jesus, is calling us up to heaven.

PHILIPPIANS 3:13-14 NLT

❖

Easy come, easy go,
but steady diligence pays off.

PROVERBS 13:11 MSG

❖

Since we are surrounded by such a huge crowd of witnesses
to the life of faith, let us strip off every weight that slows us
down, especially the sin that so easily hinders our progress.
And let us run with endurance the race that God has set
before us. We do this by keeping our eyes on Jesus, on whom
our faith depends from start to finish.

HEBREWS 12:1-2 NLT

❖

Don't ever quit. Just keep it simple.

2 TIMOTHY 4:2 MSG

. . . I will pray.

Father God,

You know what I need right now? I need the energy of one of those furry toy bunnies with a drum and a battery pack that never stops. If I'm going to meet this goal in my life, I have to keep going. I can't give up. You know all about this challenge, God. I really want to accomplish this, so I'm going to need a boost! And I'm not talking about caffeine. I need diligence—and lots of it.

I feel like I'm in the middle of a race and I'm looking for the drink table. You know, the one with the big orange cooler and the people who hand you cups of water to keep you going. I need You to help me stay steady on my course. I'm holding out my hand to You for that cup.

I know You're there, God. I feel You all around me. I know I'm not alone. In this race, You're there at the beginning, the middle, and the end. With You sustaining me, I know I'll reach the finish line. So I thank You for choosing me to run this race, for giving me help along the way, and for cheering me on in the final stretch.

Amen.

God wishes each of us to work as hard as we can, holding nothing back but giving ourselves to the utmost, and when we can do no more, that is the moment when the hand of divine providence is stretched out to us and takes over.

Don Orione

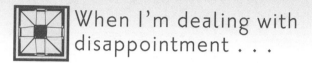# When I'm dealing with disappointment . . .

You keep track of all my sorrows.
You have collected all my tears in your bottle.
You have recorded each one in your book.

PSALM 56:8 NLT

❖

You heard their cries for help and saved them;
they were never disappointed when they sought your aid.

PSALM 22:5 TLB

❖

Unrelenting disappointment leaves you heartsick,
but a sudden good break can turn life around.

PROVERBS 13:12 MSG

❖

Why then be downcast? Why be discouraged and sad?
Hope in God! I shall yet praise him again. Yes, I shall again
praise him for his help.

PSALM 42:5 TLB

. . . I will pray.

Heavenly Father:

Letdowns are tough, God. Whether it's the letdown of a goal I didn't reach or the letdown of a loved one who really hurt me—it's a blow to my energy and my hope. Disappointment can ground me and leave me stuck in the mud. It's heartbreaking to let this disappointing experience get the best of me, but it's just so hard to dig myself free.

I'm ready to move from this situation, and I'm reaching out for encouragement and strength from You. In Your Word You remind me that I can stretch out my eagle wings and raise myself higher and higher, soaring and cascading in the freedom of hope and strength. Disappointment shouldn't keep me down, God. In this moment, my biggest dream is to rise above this muddy disappointment and soar once again.

Setbacks are inevitable. But You are always there at the beginning, middle, and end. You're right there with me, so close I can almost hear Your still, small voice saying, "Never give up. I am always with you." Be my hope and my renewed energy, and make this letdown be long gone.

I love You, God, for You are the Strength of my life.

Amen.

Out of every disappointment there is treasure.
Satan whispers, "All is lost." God says,
"Much can be gained."

Frances J. Roberts

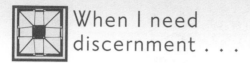

When I need discernment . . .

Give discernment to me, your servant;
then I will understand your decrees.

PSALM 119:125 NLT

❖

The word of God is living and active, . . . discerning the
thoughts and intentions of the heart.

HEBREWS 4:12 RSV

❖

Test everything. Hold on to the good.

1 THESSALONIANS 5:21

❖

O LORD, listen to my cry;
give me the discerning mind you promised.

PSALM 119:169 NLT

❖

I, Wisdom, live together with good judgment. I know where
to discover knowledge and discernment.

PROVERBS 8:12 NLT

. . . I will pray.

Almighty God,

I've got this situation in front of me, God, and I've been trying to understand the right way to deal with it. I feel like I'm a judge, like I'm sitting at my bench, wearing a black robe and holding a gavel, listening to both sides and weighing my decision. But the thing is, I don't know how to do this job. I could probably pretend to be "honorable," but the real thing? Nope, I don't know what I'm doing. So I'm calling on You, God. What do I do? What can You see that I can't?

That's what's so cool about You. You can see it all. You're seeing it from Your big-picture perspective. I need Your guidance and wisdom to lead me through. I need Your discernment so I understand the right thing to do. While I may not feel qualified, You are the best Judge ever. And I want all the decisions of my life to come from Your bench, and Your masterful discernment.

I'm going to take a deep breath, Lord, trust Your direction, and take another look at this thing. I know You're with me, and I thank You for Your brilliant direction.

Amen.

A moment's insight is sometimes worth
a life's experience.

Oliver Wendell Holmes

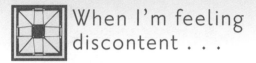# When I'm feeling discontent . . .

I have learned to be content whatever the circumstances. I know what it is to be in need, and I know what it is to have plenty. I have learned the secret of being content in any and every situation, whether well fed or hungry, whether living in plenty or in want.
PHILIPPIANS 4:11-12

❖

Godliness with contentment is great gain.
1 TIMOTHY 6:6

❖

Those who respect the LORD will live and be satisfied.
PROVERBS 19:23 NCV

❖

My soul will be satisfied as with the richest of foods; with singing lips my mouth will praise you.
PSALM 63:5

❖

From the fruit of his mouth a man's stomach is filled; with the harvest from his lips he is satisfied.
PROVERBS 18:20

. . . I will pray.

Heavenly Father,

I'm restless, dissatisfied, uneasy—there are so many names I could put on the way I feel, but I guess it all comes down to the fact that I'm not satisfied with my life as it is. I'm not content, and I'm not sure just why.

I've tried to evaluate my feelings, and I really believe my problem isn't about what I have or don't have. Why would it be? I have lots of stuff in my life—probably a lot more than most people have. And I can't really think of anything I need. So it probably isn't a matter of physical possessions.

Lord, it could be that I'm not content with my relationship with You. I know I could be closer to You, but I don't take the time. I'm sorry about that. Could it be that my restlessness and discontent hang around because I haven't invited You to be the Lord of all my life? I've just given You pieces. If that's it, help me now to surrender all to You and to find peace inside myself.

Amen.

The rarest feeling that ever lights the human face is the contentment of a loving soul.

Henry Ward Beecher

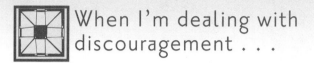

When I'm dealing with discouragement . . .

O my soul, don't be discouraged. Don't be upset.
Expect God to act! For I know that I shall again have plenty
of reason to praise him for all that he will do.
He is my help! He is my God!
PSALM 42:11 TLB

❖

Let all who are discouraged take heart.
Let us praise the Lord together,
and exalt his name.
PSALM 34:2-3 TLB

❖

Be encouraged, you who worship God.
The LORD listens to those in need.
PSALM 69:32-33 NCV

❖

When I pray, you answer me;
you encourage me by giving me the strength I need.
PSALM 138:3 NLT

. . . I will pray.

Loving Father,

Take a balloon and push all the air out, and that's how I feel right now—deflated. This situation has taken all my air, and I'm feeling pretty let down. Discouragement has grounded me.

I'm in need of a lift, Lord. Like a balloon that needs air, I need encouragement so I can fly high again. I'm looking for it everywhere: from family, friends, "little" successes, or inspiring thoughts from others that matter to me. I need that encouragement, that "air," so I can grow and fly. I'm asking You to lift me up, God. However You can, please fill me with new energy and encourage me to get up and try again.

Throughout the Bible, You show just how vital You are to our every breath. Through You, the sick were healed, the blind were able to see, and even the dead were brought back to life. Because of You, we not only live, we can thrive. So I know You can fill me up again, Lord. I'm trusting You that I will thrive once again.

Thank You for taking my discouragement and giving me a breath of Your fresh air.

Amen.

Should we feel at times disheartened and discouraged, a confiding thought, a simple movement of heart toward God will renew our powers. Whatever He may demand of us, He will give us at the moment the strength and the courage that we need.

François de Salignac de La Mothe-Fénelon

When I'm experiencing the pain of my parents divorce . . .

God will wipe away all tears from their eyes.
REVELATION 7:17 NLT

❖

God, listen! Listen to my prayer,
listen to the pain in my cries.
Don't turn your back on me
just when I need you so desperately.
Pay attention! This is a cry for help!
And hurry—this can't wait!
PSALM 102:1-2 MSG

❖

He was looked down on and passed over,
a man who suffered, who knew pain firsthand. . . .
But the fact is, it was our pains he carried.
ISAIAH 53:3-4 MSG

❖

Rescue me, O God, from my . . . pain.
Then I will praise God with my singing!
PSALM 69:29-30 TLB

. . . I will pray.

Father God,

I can't believe they're doing this. They're getting a divorce, and it's breaking my heart. Do they know how much this hurts me? They say it's the best thing for all of us. But I can't figure how this is the best thing for me. It's ruining my life. I need Your comfort, God. I know it's not my fault, but I wish I could have done something to help my parents stay together. If I knew what to do, believe me, I'd do it.

I think it's out of my control, though. I think of others who have suffered this kind of pain and grief, and all they could do was lean on You for help. I think of Job, who had so much taken from him; and Joseph, who was sold into slavery by his own brothers; and so many others who dealt with conflicts and broken relationships that were just out of their control. But You were their shoulder to cry on, lean on, and take comfort in; and I'm asking You to be my shoulder too. I'm going to need You if I'm going to get through this.

God, You are forever strong, and I thank You for being my solid Rock.

Amen.

Earth has no sorrow that heaven cannot heal.

Thomas Moore

When I have doubts . . .

Faith comes from hearing the message, and the message is heard through the word of Christ.

ROMANS 10:17

❖

Lord, when doubts fill my mind, when my heart is in turmoil, quiet me and give me renewed hope and cheer.

PSALM 94:19 TLB

❖

He has given us both his promise and his oath, two things we can completely count on, for it is impossible for God to tell a lie. Now all those who flee to him to save them can take new courage when they hear such assurances from God.

HEBREWS 6:18 TLB

❖

Be merciful to those who doubt.

JUDE 1:22 TLB

❖

Jesus [said] "Anything is possible if a person believes." The father instantly replied, "I do believe, but help me not to doubt!"

MARK 9:23-24 NLT

. . . I will pray.

Gracious God,

I love You, Lord. And I trust You. But right now I'm struggling with some doubts. I want to be firm and confident about this, but with these doubts it's hard to be strong. It's also scary to take a stand or make a move when I'm unsure of what the outcome will be. So I need Your enlightenment.

Doubting Thomas—that's the guy who needed to see the wounds in Jesus' hands and side before he could believe He was alive. He needed proof. And I can sure relate to that. But I think what I really need is the strength to trust and believe You, despite what I see or don't see. So in the midst of my doubts, I can trust You. I may have doubts, but I don't need to. Because I know You're here with me.

God, help me to be confident and sure. Help me to trust that Your hand's on my shoulder, even if I can't physically feel it. Help me to believe that You're in front of me, guiding and protecting me, even if I can't see You with my physical eyes. And thank You for hearing my doubts, and loving me while I work through them.

Amen.

Every step toward Christ kills a doubt.

Theodore Ledyard Cuyler

When I need endurance . . .

We pray that you'll have the strength to stick it out over the long haul—not the grim strength of gritting your teeth but the glory-strength God gives. It is strength that endures the unendurable and spills over into joy, thanking the Father who makes us strong enough to take part in everything bright and beautiful that he has for us.

COLOSSIANS 1:11-12 MSG

The one who endures to the end will be saved.

MATTHEW 10:22 NRSV

In our trouble God [has] comforted us—and this, too, to help you: to show you from our personal experience how God will tenderly comfort you when you undergo these same sufferings. He will give you the strength to endure.

2 CORINTHIANS 1:6-7 TLB

[Jesus said] In the good soil, these are the ones who, when they hear the word, hold it fast in an honest and good heart, and bear fruit with patient endurance.

LUKE 8:15 NRSV

. . . I will pray.

Almighty God,

There's a storm brewing, and it's headed my way. I've got a stressful time coming up. Some people love challenges like this; but I'm not so sure I've got what it takes, God. I'm going to need a great big dose of endurance to see this through. So I'm looking to You.

As a child, I always felt much safer from the storm when I was inside a strong shelter, like my house. I could sit at the window and watch the rain pour down, see the lightning split the sky's darkness with its electric force, watch the wind bend the tree branches down to the ground, and hear the thunder rumble even from miles away. It was dramatic, but as long as I was inside my house, I felt safe in the storm.

That's how I think of You, God. The storm is still scary, but when I'm sheltered by You, I can withstand it. So as I face this challenge, this storm, I'm trusting You to keep me going through it. Give me the endurance, the fortitude, to stand up and still be standing when it's over.

Thank You for being my House built on the rock . . . my Shelter in the storm . . . my Endurance.

Amen.

Nothing great was ever done without much enduring.

Catherine of Siena

When I'm being harassed by my enemies . . .

*The Lord your God is going with you! He will fight for you
against your enemies, and he will give you victory!*
DEUTERONOMY 20:4 NLT

❖

*Do not take revenge. . . . "It is mine to avenge;
I will repay," says the Lord.*
ROMANS 12:19

❖

*You [Lord] prepare a table before me
in the presence of my enemies.*
PSALM 23:5 NKJV

❖

*[The Lord] delivered me from my strong enemy, from those
who hated me—I who was helpless in their hands. On the
day when I was weakest, they attacked. But the Lord held me
steady. He led me to a place of safety, for he delights in me.*
PSALM 18:17-19 TLB

❖

*Do not be terrified, or afraid of them. The Lord your God,
who goes before you, He will fight for you.*
DEUTERONOMY 1:29-30 NKJV

. . . I will pray.

Almighty God,

Playing "Cops and Robbers" as a kid had nothing on this experience right now. I've got enemies close by, and it's definitely not as much fun as when I pretended as a child. In fact, I'm ready to run! It gives me a knot in my stomach. I wish You could take this away, God. But I have to face it, so I need Your strength to get me through.

I think about when Jesus said it was a guarantee that we would have trouble in life. But He also said not to worry because He is victorious over all our worries. That's what I want to latch on to, God: the feeling that no matter what happens, I have peace because Jesus is with me. And Jesus experienced hate much worse than I ever have. His enemies had Him killed!

I'm thankful that I'm not alone. You know what this feels like. You've been there too. You ask me to stay strong because You know it's possible to survive with my heart intact. I'm so grateful that You are behind me, helping me stand and even move forward, in spite of how my enemies are hovering over me. Thank You for being my Victory every day, in every way.

Amen.

I owe much to my friends, but all things considered,
it strikes me that I owe even more to my enemies.
The real person springs to life under a sting,
even better than under a caress.

André Gide

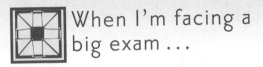

When I'm facing a big exam...

[Jesus said] I will ask the Father, and He will give you
another Helper, that He may be with you forever.

JOHN 14:16 NASB

❖

We have the mind of Christ.

1 CORINTHIANS 2:16 NRSV

❖

[Jesus said] The Helper, the Holy Spirit, whom the Father
will send in My name, He will teach you all things, and bring
to your remembrance all that I said to you. Peace I leave with
you; My peace I give to you; not as the world gives do I give
to you. Do not let your heart be troubled, nor let it be fearful.

JOHN 14:26-27 NASB

❖

You have dealt well with Your servant,
O LORD, according to Your word.
Teach me good judgment and knowledge,
For I believe Your commandments.

PSALM 119:65-66 NKJV

. . . I will pray.

Mighty Lord,

It's coming—the big day. It's marked in red on my calendar: "Big Exam," so I won't forget about it. I'd like to snap my fingers and have it magically be the day after exam day. But I'm studying hard, making sure I've got all the material I need to know. Even so, I'm anxious and stressed out about how I'll do. Anticipating this big day makes my stomach turn.

In school, my teachers tell me everything I'll need to know for the exam. They say things like, "If you've understood everything I told you, you're going to do just fine." But I still need something more. I need You, Lord—Your presence and Your peace. I need You to put Your hand on my mind and help me remember everything I need to, to do well on this exam. Calm my nerves and help me think clearly. And on the big day, before I even write my name, I'm going to bow my head again and ask You for a sharp mind and a calm demeanor. Then I'll take a deep breath and do the best that I can do.

Thank You, Lord, for helping me do my best.

Amen.

As knowledge increases, wonder deepens.

Charles Morgan

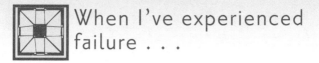

When I've experienced failure . . .

I am waiting for you, O LORD.
You must answer for me, O Lord my God.
I prayed, "Don't let my enemies gloat over me
or rejoice at my downfall."
PSALM 38:15-16 NLT

❖

I let it all out;
I said, "I'll make a clean breast of my failures to GOD."
Suddenly the pressure was gone—my guilt dissolved,
my sin disappeared.
PSALM 32:5 MSG

❖

My protection and success come from God alone.
PSALM 62:7 TLB

❖

Let the Lord our God favor us and give us success.
PSALM 90:17 TLB

❖

We know that God causes all things to work together for good
to those who love God, to those who are called according to
His purpose.
ROMANS 8:28 NASB

. . . I will pray.

Merciful God,

I feel like painting a big L on my forehead and sitting in a corner. That's pretty bad, isn't it? I was so sure of myself—but I messed up. I couldn't do what I thought I could do. I failed—big-time.

It's hard to forgive myself and start again. People tell me that it's okay, everyone fails sometime, and that I need to try again. But I'm not so sure. I feel like I'm paralyzed—frozen in place. What if I fail again . . . and again . . . and again? What if people start to think of me as a big loser who can't do anything right?

I give You all my failures, Lord, and I give You one thing more—my fear of failing again. I ask You to help me, forgive me, help me to forgive myself, and inspire me to place my trust in Your strength and success rather than in my past failures.

Thank You for clearing this road and helping me begin again with light and warmth in my heart. You're a God of second chances.

Amen.

A failure is not someone who has tried and failed;
it is someone who has given up trying and resigned
himself to failure; it is not a condition, but an attitude.

Sydney J. Harris

When I need faith . . .

Without faith it is impossible to please Him,
for he who comes to God must believe that He is,
and that He is a rewarder of those who diligently seek Him.
HEBREWS 11:6 NKJV

❖

We walk by faith, not by sight.
2 CORINTHIANS 5:7 NASB

❖

Your faith is growing more and more, and the love that every
one of you has for each other is increasing.
2 THESSALONIANS 1:3 NCV

❖

None [of those] who have faith in God will ever be
disgraced for trusting him.
PSALM 25:3 TLB

❖

[Jesus said] Do not fear, only believe.
MARK 5:36 RSV

. . . I will pray.

Gracious God,

Some kind of superhero power would be nice right now, like the ability to see into the future. If I could know the outcome of every move I make before I actually make it, wow, that would be cool! But I'm not a superhero, and I can't see a whole lot right now, and I do have questions. Questions about what's going to happen next in my life. Questions about where You are in all of this. And I don't have answers.

I need faith, God. I need to believe that even though I can't see the road ahead, You are there. I need to know that even though I can't feel You physically holding my hand, You've never let go of me. I want to be spiritually strong, so take my desire and turn it into an unwavering faith in Your goodness, Your direction, and Your presence in all of life.

I can feel my strength returning, Lord, and I thank You for transforming my feeble heart into a faithful soul. I don't need to be a superhero. I just need to stand and walk in Your ways, knowing You are always there.

Amen.

Faith does not mean believing without evidence.
It means believing in realities that go beyond sense
and sight—for which a totally different sort of
evidence is required.

John Baillie

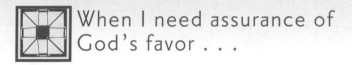

When I need assurance of God's favor . . .

I tell you, now is the time of God's favor.
2 Corinthians 6:2

✣

I entreated Your favor with my whole heart;
Be merciful to me according to Your word.
Psalm 119:58 NKJV

✣

Let your favor shine again upon your servant;
save me just because you are so kind!
Psalm 31:16 TLB

✣

His anger lasts a moment; his favor lasts for life!
Psalm 30:5 TLB

✣

Keep me as the apple of your eye.
Psalm 17:8

✣

May the favor of the Lord our God rest upon us.
Psalm 90:17

. . . I will pray.

Loving Father,

I've been pretty down lately, but someone told me that I should cheer up because You pour out Your favor on us. I couldn't help but wonder what favor he was talking about. Is it like when I give a friend a ride home or work an extra day so someone can have time off for some important event?

When I started asking around and looking up stuff in the Bible, I could see that it's not just doing people favors, but just favoring them in general—the way a teacher always gives you the benefit of the doubt or extra time on homework when you need it. That means You give me breaks—little and big—just because You like me.

Thank You, Lord, for favoring me. You may not know—actually, You being God, You surely do know—how much I need that right now. And I've been looking around me, and it's true—I can see You helping me out, speaking up for me. That means more to me than I can express in words. Thank You, Lord.

Amen.

Measure not God's love and favor by your own feeling. The sun shines as clearly in the darkest day as it does in the brightest. The difference is not in the sun, but in some clouds.

Richard Sibbs

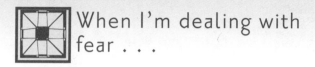 When I'm dealing with
fear . . .

God hath not given us the spirit of fear; but of power,
and of love, and of a sound mind.

2 TIMOTHY 1:7 KJV

I, the LORD your God,
hold your right hand;
it is I who say to you, "Fear not,
I will help you."

ISAIAH 41:13 RSV

❖

Fear not, for I am with you,
be not dismayed, for I am your God;
I will strengthen you, I will help you,
I will uphold you with my victorious right hand.

ISAIAH 41:10 RSV

❖

[Jesus said] Peace I leave with you; my peace I give you.
I do not give to you as the world gives. Do not let your hearts
be troubled and do not be afraid.

JOHN 14:27

. . . I will pray.

Almighty God,

It would be so great if, for just one day, I could walk around without fear. It is always there, jabbing me in the gut, getting me rattled, making me miserable, cheating me out of my life. And I don't have any idea what to do about it.

I've read that I'm supposed to face my fears—so I tried that. All I can say for sure is that I was no match. One look and my fear became terror. Now I see things everywhere; dangers real or imagined stalk me every minute of every day. You are my only hope, Lord. I could never tell anyone else about this. I'm too afraid.

Father, I know it isn't Your desire for me to live in fear. You love me and want me to be free to live my life to the fullest and walk in Your will and purpose. And if it's Your will for me to be free, it must also be Your desire to deliver me from my fears and give me the victory over them. Right now, right here, I surrender my life, my fears, my very self to You. I place my full trust in Your ability to protect me. Do Your work of grace in my life.

Amen.

God incarnate is the end of fear; and the heart
that realizes that he is in the midst . . . will be quiet in
the midst of alarm.

F. B. Meyer

When I need to forgive . . .

Get along with each other, and forgive each other.
If someone does wrong to you, forgive that person because
the Lord forgave you.
COLOSSIANS 3:13 NCV

❖

[Jesus said] Judge not, and you will not be judged;
condemn not, and you will not be condemned; forgive,
and you will be forgiven.
LUKE 6:37 RSV

❖

[Jesus said] Whenever you stand praying, forgive,
if you have anything against anyone, so that your Father who
is in heaven will also forgive you your transgressions.
But if you do not forgive, neither will your Father who
is in heaven forgive your transgressions.
MARK 11:25-26 NASB

❖

Peter came to [Jesus] and asked, "Lord, how often should I
forgive someone who sins against me? Seven times?"
"No!" Jesus replied, "seventy times seven!"
MATTHEW 18:21-22 NLT

. . . I will pray.

Merciful God,

The words went in like a knife—so cruel, so painful, so unnecessary. And after that, this person I once thought was my friend, this person I once thought cared about me, this person I trusted, just walked away. Now, my so-called friend wants things to be the way they were, wants everything to be just fine between us, wants me to forgive if he offended me in any way. I can hardly believe it.

It seems so unfair. I'm the one who got hurt and now I'm the one who has to do the right thing and forgive. That person hasn't suffered at all—I don't think he's really sorry or even realizes what he did to me. He just gets to go on with his life like nothing even happened, while I'm being asked to forget that I have this big hole in my gut.

Lord, I could never get past this if it wasn't for what I read in the Bible about the things that were done to You—and how You were betrayed by someone You thought was Your friend. Because of that, Lord, I know that You've done the hard thing You're asking me to do—forgive. Help me as I strive to follow Your example.

Amen.

Humanity is never so beautiful as when praying
for forgiveness or else forgiving another.

Jean Paul Richter

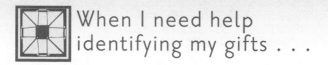

When I need help identifying my gifts . . .

You created my inmost being;
you knit me together in my mother's womb.
I praise you because I am fearfully and wonderfully made;
your works are wonderful,
I know that full well.

PSALM 139:13-14

❖

We are God's [own] handiwork (His workmanship),
recreated in Christ Jesus, . . . that we may do those good
works which God predestined (planned beforehand) for us
[taking paths which He prepared ahead of time], that we
should walk in them.

EPHESIANS 2:10 AMP

❖

God gives us many kinds of special abilities, but it is the same
Holy Spirit who is the source of them all. There are different
kinds of service to God, but it is the same Lord we are
serving. There are many ways in which God works in our
lives, but it is the same God who does the work in and
through all of us who are his.

1 CORINTHIANS 12:4-6 TLB

. . . I will pray.

Gracious God,

I love presents. I love seeing them wrapped in paper and ribbon. I love the anticipation of wondering what's inside, what wonderful surprise waits for me to claim it as my own.

The Bible says that You have given me gifts and talents. You've wrapped them up in Your love and placed them inside me, where I will find them one by one and open them. Your Word says that they are unique, created just for me—gifts designed to help me praise and worship You.

Lord, I ask for Your help as I seek to discover the gifts and abilities You've given me. Help me not to give up too easily or settle for something less than Your best. I also ask that You open my mind to those gifts that are less obvious, more difficult to identify.

I can't wait to see what You have for me, Lord. I know each and every gift will be one that will be pleasing in Your eyes. Thank You, Lord, for Your good and perfect gifts.

Amen.

God gives to every man the virtue, temper, understanding, and taste that lifts him into life, and lets him fall just in the niche he was ordained to fill.

William Cowper

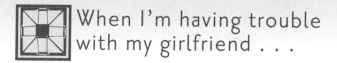

When I'm having trouble with my girlfriend . . .

He guides me in paths of righteousness
for his name's sake.
PSALM 23:3

❖

In all your ways acknowledge Him,
And He shall direct your paths.
PROVERBS 3:6 NKJV

❖

The God of patience and consolation grant you to be
likeminded one toward another according to Christ Jesus: that
ye may with one mind and one mouth glorify God, even the
Father of our Lord Jesus Christ.
ROMANS 15:5-6 KJV

❖

Only conduct yourselves in a manner worthy of the gospel of
Christ, so that whether I come and see you or remain absent,
I will hear of you that you are standing firm in one spirit,
with one mind striving together for the faith of the gospel.
PHILIPPIANS 1:27 NASB

. . . I will pray.

Loving Father,

I'm having some problems in my relationship with my girlfriend, and I sure could use a helping hand. I'm feeling uncertain and need Your guidance.

God, Your Word says that You help direct us on the right path all through life. That's where I want to be right now—walking close to You, listening to Your instructions, and feeling safe in Your presence. Help me, Lord, to walk on the path You've designed for me.

Father, I pray that my girlfriend would want to be close to You, just as I desire to be close to You. And that we would be in harmony about how to treat our relationship and ensure that it is pleasing to You.

Give me wisdom to deal with this relationship, Lord. Show me how to do and say those things that will honor You and honor her. Whatever our relationship ends up being in the weeks and months ahead, help us to be united in our desire to be a blessing to You and to each other.

Amen.

If you live by the same values Jesus had, then you won't have to wonder if your relationships will be God-honoring and fulfilling.

Anonymous

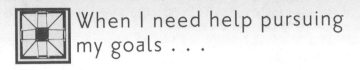

When I need help pursuing my goals . . .

If you are willing and obedient,
you shall eat the good of the land.
ISAIAH 1:19 NRSV

❖

LORD, you are mine!
I promise to obey your words! . . .
I pondered the direction of my life,
and I turned to follow your statutes.
PSALM 119:57, 59 NLT

❖

Keep your heart with all vigilance;
for from it flow the springs of life. . . .
Let your eyes look directly forward,
and your gaze be straight before you.
Take heed to the path of your feet,
then all your ways will be sure.
Do not swerve to the right or to the left.
PROVERBS 4:23, 25-27 RSV

❖

The LORD says, "I will guide you along the best pathway for
your life. I will advise you and watch over you."
PSALM 32:8 NLT

. . . I will pray.

Gracious God,

I've got a lot of goals—some big, some small, some that will be more difficult to obtain than others. I also know I'm motivated, and we both know that when I sink my teeth into something, I'm like a tiger. I don't let go until I get the job done. There's a question I've been asking myself though, and it's one I need to ask You right now: what if the goals I've locked onto aren't the ones that will help me fulfill Your will for my life?

The last thing I want, Father, is to get to the end of my life and realize that my goals weren't Your goals and that my life had been a waste. So, before I tackle these, I'm offering them to You. Show me if any of my goals are going to take me in the wrong direction, away from Your perfect will. I'm thinking it will be tough if I have to make major adjustments, but I'll make them. More than anything I want to be all that You've created me to be.

Thank You, Lord, for Your promise to lead and guide me to a life of true success.

Amen.

My goal is God himself, not joy nor peace,
Nor even blessing, but himself, my God,
'Tis his to lead me there, not mine but his
At any cost, dear Lord, by any road!

E. Brook

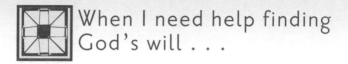

When I need help finding God's will . . .

"I know what I am planning for you," says the LORD.
"I have good plans for you, not plans to hurt you.
I will give you hope and a good future."
JEREMIAH 29:11 NCV

❖

As your plan unfolds, even the simple can understand it.
PSALM 119:130 TLB

❖

David said, "All these plans were written with
the LORD guiding me. He helped me understand everything
in the plans."
1 CHRONICLES 28:19 NCV

❖

[Jesus said] Anyone who does God's will is my brother,
and my sister, and my mother.
MARK 3:35 TLB

❖

[Not in your own strength] for it is God Who is all the while
effectually at work in you [energizing and creating in you the
power and desire], both to will and to work for His
good pleasure and satisfaction and delight.
PHILIPPIANS 2:13 AMP

. . . I will pray.

Almighty God,

Sometimes knowing Your will for me seems like a puzzle. Some pieces are in place, some are waiting to be placed, and some . . . well, I just can't seem to figure out where they fit. Wouldn't it be great if You could just write the answers on a billboard or in a letter or something? Maybe You could package it all up in a dream for me. But I know that's not how You usually work.

Father, I don't know how to sort out the puzzle of Your will for me, but I do know You have the answers. During our times together, help me to clear away the uncertainty and identify those missing pieces and where they fit. I know that some of the pieces aren't meant to be revealed right now—that they will play out in my life over time. For those I ask that You will help me trust You to lead me along the way.

Thank You, Lord, for being so invested in my life. It's wonderful to know that You've created me for a purpose, and I look forward to discovering that purpose as You reveal it to me.

Amen.

Be simple; take our Lord's hand and
walk through things.

Father Andrew

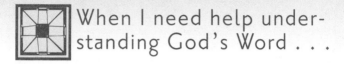# When I need help understanding God's Word . . .

*[Jesus said] The words that I speak to you are spirit,
and they are life.*

JOHN 6:63 NKJV

*Give me understanding, that I may observe Your law
And keep it with all my heart.*

PSALM 119:34 NASB

*If you want better insight and discernment, and are searching
for them as you would for lost money or hidden treasure, then
wisdom will be given you and knowledge of God himself; you
will soon learn the importance of reverence for the Lord and
of trusting him. For the Lord grants wisdom! His every word
is a treasure of knowledge and understanding.*

PROVERBS 2:3-6 TLB

Lead me in your truth, and teach me.

PSALM 25:5 NRSV

❖

*Open my eyes that I may see
wonderful things in your law.*

PSALM 119:18

. . . I will pray.

Merciful God,

I never really thought about the Bible being Your Word—not until lately. I guess I just thought about it as another book, a holy one, but a book just the same. But now, thinking of it as Your actual words—as in a letter or a speech—changes everything about the Bible for me. It makes it personal. I want to read it again in a new way and learn all I can about You.

The trouble is that sometimes I just don't understand what You're trying to tell me. The words are old and some parts don't make any sense to me at all. Still I know Your message is there, waiting for me to figure it out so I can get to know You better. Of course, the other problem is that my understanding is limited, certainly not equal to the job of fully discerning the thoughts and intentions of Almighty God!

Father, I know it's Your will for me to read and understand Your Word, so I'm asking for extra help. When I get to those hard-to-figure-out places, give me special insight. I realize even my entire lifetime is not enough to fully grasp all the treasures of Your Word, but I'm ready to start the journey now. Thanks for teaching me.

Amen.

Come, Holy Ghost, for moved by thee
The prophets wrote and spoke;
Unlock the truth, thyself the key,
Unseal the sacred book.

John Calvin

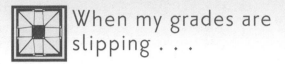

When my grades are slipping . . .

We do not enjoy being disciplined. It is painful, but later,
after we have learned from it, we have peace,
because we start living in the right way.
HEBREWS 12:11 NCV

❖

The proverbs of Solomon son of David, king of Israel:
for attaining wisdom and discipline;
for understanding words of insight;
for acquiring a disciplined and prudent life,
doing what is right.
PROVERBS 1:1-3

❖

I know, O LORD, that your decisions are fair;
you disciplined me because I needed it.
Now let your unfailing love comfort me.
PSALM 119:75-76 NLT

❖

The road to life is a disciplined life.
PROVERBS 10:17 MSG

. . . I will pray.

Gracious God,

I wish all I had to do was study—but You know that's only a part of being in school. There are all the other things like sports and friends and my job. With all that going on, something is going to suffer, and right now, it's my grades.

Lord, when I look at the big picture, I know my grades are the most important thing, that all the other stuff has to come second. But in the moment, when my friends are wanting me to go someplace or my favorite show is on TV, or I just don't feel like getting out of bed, my priorities seem to get all mixed up. That's where I need Your help. Give me the self-control I need to say no to distractions and yes to study.

Thank You, Lord, for giving me a good mind that—with a little hard work—can do what it needs to do. Forgive me when I dishonor that by being irresponsible with my schoolwork. And thank You for helping me when I get to one of those subjects I have trouble with. I want to honor You by being a good student.

Amen.

Some people regard discipline as a chore.
For me, it is a kind of order that sets me free to fly.
Julie Andrews

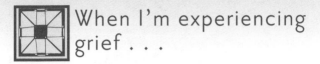# When I'm experiencing grief . . .

Be gracious to me, O LORD, for I am in distress;
My eye is wasted away from grief, my soul and my body also.
PSALM 31:9 NASB

❖

I weep with grief;
encourage me by your word.
PSALM 119:28 NLT

❖

[Jesus said] Truly, truly, I say to you, that you will weep and
lament, . . . but your grief will be turned into joy.
JOHN 16:20 NASB

❖

I say, "It is my grief
that the right hand of the Most High has changed."
I will call to mind the deeds of the LORD;
yea, I will remember thy wonders of old.
PSALM 77:10-11 RSV

. . . I will pray.

Father God,

My heart is broken in two. I'm not even sure I can find the words to express how I feel right now—good thing You know me and can see inside my mind. I always knew something like this could happen. People die; that's a fact of life. But somehow, in my silly head, I never thought I would lose someone who meant so much to me. Now I feel lost, like I'm floating in the ocean and every breath could be my last.

Help me, Lord. Reach out to me with Your comfort. I need it so much right now. My friends and family try to help, but they can touch me only on the outside—they can't do anything about my heart.

I'm so glad You see and understand all the things that happen in my life. I don't have to go looking for You and try to explain the whole situation—You just know instantly. And it's good to know that I'll never lose You. You won't die or turn Your back on me. You will always be here, giving me just what I need when I need it. Thank You, Lord, for being my Rescuer when I'm all alone and drifting in the ocean of my life.

Amen.

Grief can be your servant, helping you to feel more compassion for others who hurt.

Robert Harold Schuller

When I need guidance . . .

Teach me Your way, O Lord;
lead me in a straight path.
PSALM 27:11

❖

We humans keep brainstorming options and plans,
but God's purpose prevails.
PROVERBS 19:21 MSG

❖

The Lord says, "I will guide you along the best pathway for
your life. I will advise you and watch over you."
PSALM 32:8 NLT

❖

He leadeth me in the paths of righteousness
for his name's sake.
PSALM 23:3 KJV

❖

If you leave God's paths and go astray, you will hear a Voice
behind you say, "No, this is the way; walk here."
ISAIAH 30:21 TLB

. . . I will pray.

Heavenly Father,

This decision is like a fork in the road. I just don't know which way to go. I've already tried asking people for directions. They offered what they could—but no one is willing to tell me what to do here. They all seem to be determined that I make this decision myself.

Well . . . if it's time to start making big decisions on my own, then I also want to start out on the right foot by asking for Your help—to be my Friend and Guide—not only for this decision, but for all the decisions I will face in the future. I believe that together we can get me on the right path!

Thank You, Lord, for putting me on the road to Your perfect will in the first place. And I believe with all my heart that You are going to lead me all the way to my destination, around every turn and over, under, or through every obstacle. All You ask is that I stop and listen carefully when I'm unsure which way to go—listen for Your voice to show me the way. I'm listening, Lord.

Amen.

Abraham did not know the way,
but he knew the Guide.

Lee Roberson

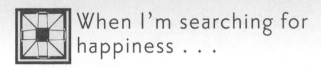# When I'm searching for happiness . . .

[Jesus said] You're blessed when you're content with just who you are—no more, no less. That's the moment you find yourselves proud owners of everything that can't be bought.

MATTHEW 5:5 MSG

❖

[Jesus said] If you're content to simply be yourself, your life will count for plenty.

MATTHEW 23:12 MSG

❖

LORD, you have made me happy by what you have done; I will sing for joy about what your hands have done.

PSALM 92:4 NCV

❖

You have made known to me the path of life; you will fill me with joy in your presence, with eternal pleasures at your right hand.

PSALM 16:11

. . . I will pray.

Loving God,

I can laugh with friends, smile at people at the mall, and basically, everything seems fine. But I've got a secret: I want the kind of life that makes me smile when no one is looking. I'd like to have a taste of real happiness.

I see a lot of people who are concerned with how they look. They want to be attractive, popular, talented, or cool. They work so hard at it, but when they get it, they don't seem happy. There's always one more little imperfection to fix. Other people are always wanting to get their hands on some new toy, new car, new clothes, whatever. But as soon as they get what they've been after, the happiness melts away and they go after something else.

I want to be happy with myself and my life, just the way I am. I mean, I want to improve myself, but not for others. I want to please You and be at peace with who You've created me to be. I don't need to be attractive, famous, or rich. I just want to smile when no one is looking, because being with You makes me happy.

Amen.

God cannot give us happiness and peace apart
from himself, because it is not there.
There is no such thing.

C. S. Lewis

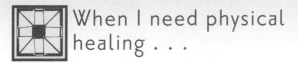

When I need physical healing . . .

They cried to the LORD in their trouble,
and he saved them from their distress;
he sent out his word and healed them.

PSALM 107:19-20 NRSV

❖

He took the punishment, and that made us whole.
Through his bruises we get healed.

ISAIAH 53:5 MSG

❖

You shall serve the LORD your God, and He will bless
your bread and your water. And I will take sickness
away from the midst of you.

EXODUS 23:25 NKJV

❖

I am the LORD who heals you.

EXODUS 15:26 NLT

❖

Heal me, O LORD, and I shall be healed; save me,
and I shall be saved.

JEREMIAH 17:14 KJV

. . . I will pray.

Gracious God,

It's not just about the pain. My physical condition has affected my life in so many ways. It affects my time, and the way I do things. And it's more difficult to take on the daily events of life. It's become a main focus of my life—and that's exactly what I don't want, Lord. I don't want this infirmity to have power over me. I need Your healing touch.

I remember the woman who touched Jesus' clothes. She just knew that if she could make some kind of contact, she would be better off. She might be healed. And she was right! She reached out for You, and with one touch her life was transformed. That's what I need, God—a transforming touch. So I'm here, waiting, trusting, in faith believing that Your healing hands will reach out with compassion and love and change my life forever.

Thank You for the strength You give me every day, no matter what I'm facing. Thank You for the right You've given me to come into Your presence and present my requests to You. More than anything, I believe that You want what's best for me—You always have and You always will.

Amen.

Our Substitute bore both our sins and our sicknesses
that we might be delivered from them.

F. F. Bosworth

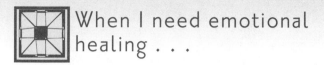

When I need emotional healing . . .

He will not break the bruised reed, nor quench the
dimly burning flame. He will encourage the fainthearted,
those tempted to despair.

ISAIAH 42:3 TLB

❖

Those who discover these words live, really live;
body and soul, they're bursting with health.

PROVERBS 4:22 MSG

❖

Weeping may remain for a night,
but rejoicing comes in the morning.

PSALM 30:5

❖

He will wipe away every tear from their eyes;
and there will no longer be any death;
there will no longer be any mourning, or crying, or pain.

REVELATION 21:4 NASB

❖

God blesses those who are kind to the poor. . . . He nurses
them when they are sick, and soothes their pains and worries.

PSALM 41:1, 3 TLB

. . . I will pray.

Heavenly Father,

I've been in kind of a cocoon lately—hiding out, trying to fix my emotional wounds. But I'm finding that I can't do it on my own. I can try to talk with others about what I'm going through, but it still hurts, God. I need Your intervention to help me rise above my pain.

I hope that as I keep working through this, I'll eventually see some light. Sometimes we need time to lie low, and then we need to start pushing our way out of our cocoons. I've been pushing, but I need You, God, to grow and develop my wings. Then I'll need Your strength to help me give that final big push before I fly free, away from this hurt.

Your ways are perfect, Lord, and Your thoughts are much higher than mine. I know You can take this pain I'm going through and use it for my good. With Your help, the little hurt person I was when I went inside this cocoon will emerge strong and healthy and ready to face life again. Thank You, Lord.

Amen.

Psychotherapy will put a Band-Aid on the gash; but for healing, men's lives must be changed from within.

Raymond J. Larson

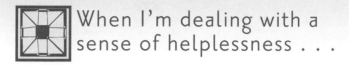

When I'm dealing with a sense of helplessness . . .

GOD takes the side of the helpless;
when I was at the end of my rope, he saved me.
PSALM 116:6 MSG

❖

You have been a defense for the helpless,
A defense for the needy in his distress.
ISAIAH 25:4 NASB

❖

Lord, because I am poor and helpless, please remember me.
You are my helper and savior. My God, do not wait.
PSALM 40:17 NCV

❖

This is what the LORD says:
"In the time of my favor I will answer you,
and in the day of salvation I will help you."
ISAIAH 49:8

❖

Don't be afraid, for I am with you. Do not be dismayed, for I
am your God. I will strengthen you. I will help you. I will
uphold you with my victorious right hand.
ISAIAH 41:10 NLT

. . . I will pray.

Dear Lord,

When life is going my way, I feel strong and invincible—as if I deserve the credit for it. Carefree and happy, I am confident that "fortune" has smiled on me and my mountaintop existence will never be disturbed.

But when things start to fall apart, so do I. I fall into confusion and flounder around like a fish out of water. At times like those, I feel helpless and out of control. It doesn't even have to be about me. I feel equally helpless when someone else is in deep water. While I should be throwing him or her a lifeline, I'm running in circles on the shore, waving my arms and shouting, "Somebody help!"

Lord, can You help me to keep my head when everyone around me is falling apart? Can You teach me courage in the face of fear, strength when I feel weak, and faith to believe that things will get better? Give me the wisdom to know what to do to help, instead of always being part of the problem. Forgive me for failing to see You as the Source of my good times and my Helper during my bad times.

Amen.

Prayer and helplessness are inseparable. Only he who is helpless can truly pray. Your helplessness is your best prayer. It calls from your heart to the heart of God with greater effect than all your uttered pleas.

Ole Hallesby

When I need hope . . .

You are my hope;
O Lord GOD, You are my confidence from my youth.
PSALM 71:5 NASB

❖

Why are you cast down, O my soul,
and why are you disquieted within me?
Hope in God; for I shall again praise him,
my help and my God.
PSALM 43:5 RSV

❖

May the God of hope fill you with all joy and peace as you
trust in him, so that you may overflow with hope by the
power of the Holy Spirit.
ROMANS 15:13

❖

I would have lost heart, unless I had believed
That I would see the goodness of the LORD
In the land of the living.
PSALM 27:13 NKJV

. . . I will pray.

Heavenly Father,

I'm young. Some people say my generation is the hope for the future. If we are, I don't see how we can ever overcome all the evil in the world or even find a way to hold things together for a little longer. All I see in the papers tells me that things are getting a lot worse rather than better. This world needs more hope than I can give.

I'm coming to You with this because I really don't know where else to turn. I need a good, solid dose of hope right now. I need Your assurance that Your will is still being done here on earth. I feel confident that You can show me how I can make a difference—if not on a grand scale, maybe just in my group of friends and in my community.

Lord, open my heart as You have for so many before me— those who suffered without ever giving up hope that You would turn their tears to joy, those who kept on working against all odds without losing hope that their efforts would one day be rewarded. I want to hope in You, Lord.

Amen.

Everything that is done in the world is done by hope.

Martin Luther

When I need a job . . .

*Let the thief no longer steal, but rather let him labor,
doing honest work with his hands, so that he may be able
to give to those in need.*

EPHESIANS 4:28 RSV

❖

*That every man who eats and drinks sees good in
all his labor—it is the gift of God.*

ECCLESIASTES 3:13 NASB

❖

*You will eat the fruit of your labor;
blessings and prosperity will be yours.*

PSALM 128:2

❖

*It is good and fitting for one to eat and drink, and to enjoy
the good of all his labor in which he toils under the sun all the
days of his life which God gives him; for it is his heritage. As
for every man to whom God has given riches and wealth, and
given him power to eat of it, to receive his heritage and rejoice
in his labor—this is the gift of God.*

ECCLESIASTES 5:18-19 NKJV

. . . I will pray.

My Lord,

I can't believe it. All of a sudden, getting a job has become a big deal, and I have no idea where to start. Retail sales, food service, yard work, phone sales—I would never have guessed there would be so many choices. And guess what, I'm not good at any of them.

Everywhere I've gone, the first thing they ask is what experience and skills I have. That's easy—none. So what am I supposed to do? Make something up? I'm really getting frustrated, and I need Your help.

I'm willing to work hard and do whatever my employer tells me. But first I need some help deciding what I want to do—what I can do—what I'm even interested in. Then, I'm going to have to figure out how much I can work without ruining my grades and having no life at all.

Thank You, Lord, for helping me sort it all out and find the right opportunity to fit my needs. And thanks for making it all right for me to come to You about everything in my life.

Amen.

Each individual has his own kind of living assigned to him by the Lord as a sort of sentry post.

John Calvin

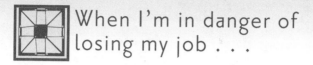

When I'm in danger of losing my job . . .

You will keep in perfect peace all who trust in you,
whose thoughts are fixed on you!
ISAIAH 26:3 NLT

❖

They are not afraid of evil tidings;
their hearts are firm, secure in the LORD.
Their hearts are steady, they will not be afraid.
PSALM 112:7-8 NRSV

❖

I have set the LORD always before me;
Because He is at my right hand I shall not be moved.
Therefore my heart is glad, and my glory rejoices;
My flesh also will rest in hope.
PSALM 16:8-9 NKJV

❖

"I know the plans that I have for you," declares the LORD,
"plans for welfare and not for calamity to give you a future
and a hope."
JEREMIAH 29:11 NASB

. . . I will pray.

Dear Father,

I realize that all kinds of people lose their jobs for all kinds of reasons all the time. I just never thought I would have to worry about being one of them. I never dreamed that things that seem so insignificant to me could make such a difference to my boss. For the most part, I try to work really hard.

Lord, I want to be pleasing to You and be a responsible person at work. And I can see now that means tending to the little things—following instructions, being on time, being courteous, being more flexible with the schedule, and making sure that I'm doing a good job.

I've learned a big lesson, Lord. Good jobs aren't easy to find. If I do lose my present job, I ask You to help me find a new one. You can be sure that I won't take it lightly again. I'll treat my job like a gift rather than an irritation—something I have to do. Thank You for leading me to someone who will give me a second chance to do my best with Your help.

Amen.

If God maintains sun and planets in bright and ordered beauty, he can keep us.

F. B. Meyer

When I want to know God
better . . .

*[Jesus said] This is eternal life: [it means] to know (to
perceive, recognize, become acquainted with, and understand)
You, the only true and real God, and [likewise] to know
Him, Jesus [as the] Christ (the Anointed One, the Messiah),
Whom You have sent.*

JOHN 17:3 AMP

❖

*In the past you did not know God. You were slaves to gods
that were not real. But now you know the true God.
Really, it is God who knows you.*

GALATIANS 4:8-9 NCV

❖

*This is how we may discern [daily, by experience] that we
are coming to know Him [to perceive, recognize, understand,
and become better acquainted with Him]: if we keep
(bear in mind, observe, practice) His teachings
(precepts, commandments).*

1 JOHN 2:3 AMP

❖

*I want to know Christ and the power that raised
him from the dead.*

PHILIPPIANS 3:10 NCV

. . . I will pray.

Father God,

I run into someone every once in a while who speaks as if he or she hangs out with You—as if the two of you are best buds. Those people know things about You that amaze and fascinate me; and believe it or not, I find myself wishing I were in their shoes.

As You know, I've never had any interest in reading the Bible. Some parts sound like a fairy tale—a little unrealistic—while the rest sounds like a school handbook, full of rules and regulations. I've never much liked going to church either. I get really bored at times. But the idea of knowing You, well, that's different; that actually sounds exciting to me!

So, Lord, how can I get to know You better? I've heard people say that I'm wrong about the Bible being a rule book. They say it is more like a letter. I suppose if I read it like a letter, instead of like an instruction manual, I might get more out of it. It's worth a try. After all, that would be a good way for us to spend time together, wouldn't it? Okay, I'll get started right away. Thanks for giving me a chance to know You.

Amen.

Oh, the fullness, pleasure, sheer excitement of
knowing God on Earth!

Jim Elliot

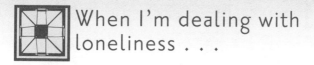# When I'm dealing with loneliness . . .

I meditate on You in the night watches. . . .
My soul follows close behind You;
Your right hand upholds me.
PSALM 63:6, 8 NKJV

❖

I am continually with You;
You have taken hold of my right hand.
PSALM 73:23 NASB

❖

[Jesus said] I am with you always, to the close of the age.
MATTHEW 28:20 RSV

❖

[Jesus said] I no longer call you servants, because a servant
does not know what his master is doing. But I call you
friends, because I have made known to you everything
I heard from my Father.
JOHN 15:15 NCV

. . . I will pray.

Dear Father,

Just when I thought I was part of the group, I found out that I was left out of something. It really hurts. Not that I really wanted to go anyway, but it would have been nice to have been invited. It just points out to me again that I don't have any friends—no one to talk to and no one to care.

Oh sure, my family cares, but that doesn't really count because my family pretty much has to like me. I'm just having a lot of trouble dealing with the loneliness in my life right now.

It helps a little knowing that Jesus felt lonely, too, at times. I suppose when He felt alone, He prayed. I guess that's why I'm praying, because that is the only thing I can do that seems to help. You are always there for me, Lord. Not necessarily in the way I wanted, but always in some way—in Your way.

So I'm asking now, Lord, could You relieve this feeling of loneliness that is hounding me right now? Take away the hurt and help me see myself through Your eyes. Thank You, Lord, for loving me and being my Friend for my whole life.

Amen.

In every man there is a loneliness, an inner chamber of peculiar life into which God only can enter.

George MacDonald

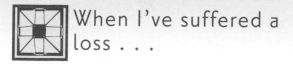# When I've suffered a loss . . .

God of all healing counsel! He comes alongside us when
we go through hard times, and before you know it, he brings
us alongside someone else who is going through hard times
so that we can be there for that person just as
God was there for us.

2 CORINTHIANS 1:3-4 MSG

❖

This is my comfort in my affliction,
That Your word has revived me. . . .
I have remembered Your ordinances from of old, O LORD,
And comfort myself.

PSALM 119:50, 52 NASB

❖

Be merciful to me, O LORD, for I am in distress;
my eyes grow weak with sorrow,
my soul and my body with grief. . . .
But I trust in You, O LORD; . . .
I say, "You are my God."
My times are in your hands.

PSALM 31:9, 14-15

. . . I will pray.

Heavenly Father,

Can You help me? I have a huge hole in my heart. I just lost someone really close to me, and I haven't ever felt like this before.

Just days ago, I was cruising along and everything was wonderful. Out of nowhere, it seems, my whole world fell apart, and I came tumbling down with it. What do I do now? Where do I go with my grief? How can I face another day of sadness?

I've known other types of loss—moving away, changing schools, the death of a pet. I know the gut-twisting pain of losing a friend and the agony of losing the championship title. All of those are pretty tough to take. But this was the worst.

I guess my real question is, how can I be sure that You are still here for me when I've lost someone really important in my life? Maybe You want me to stop and take stock of all the good that remains. Lord, only You can open my heart to believe that though today is full of sadness, there are more good things ahead. I'm just glad I haven't lost You.

Amen.

Truly, it is in darkness that one finds the light, so when we are in sorrow, then this light is nearest of all to us.

Meister Eckhart

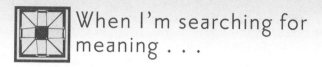

When I'm searching for meaning . . .

I concentrated with all my might, studying and exploring and seeking wisdom—the meaning of life.
ECCLESIASTES 7:25 MSG

❖

There's nothing better than being wise,
Knowing how to interpret the meaning of life.
ECCLESIASTES 8:1 MSG

❖

He determined the times set for them and the exact places where they should live.
ACTS 17:26

❖

We know that in everything God works for good with those who love him, who are called according to his purpose.
ROMANS 8:28 RSV

❖

Be strong and steady, always abounding in the Lord's work, for you know that nothing you do for the Lord is ever wasted.
1 CORINTHIANS 15:58 TLB

. . . I will pray.

Dear Father God,

Day after day, I go through the same routine. I get up, go to school, come home, do homework, watch TV, go to bed. Then I get up the next morning and start all over again. Sometimes it feels as if my life doesn't mean anything at all.

Everyone says that the brand of clothing I wear, the way I style my hair, the friends I hang out with, and the type of car I drive will give me a sense of significance. But I found out they're wrong.

I'm looking for the kind of meaning that goes deeper than that—the kind that cuts through the fads and fashions and lasts longer than the latest trend. I'm looking for what defines me as a person, what determines my future, and what I should believe in.

Lord, something tells me that You alone can give true meaning to my life. Since You are my Creator, You know more than anyone else what I was created to do and who I was created to be. I realize that I won't know the whole story until the end, but if I could get just a glimpse, it would mean a lot to me.

Amen.

Life can never be wholly dark or wholly futile once the key to its meaning is in our hands.

J. B. Phillips

When I need a miracle . . .

How we thank you, Lord!
Your mighty miracles give proof that you care.
PSALM 75:1 TLB

❖

Everyone shall stand in awe and confess the greatness of
the miracles of God; at last they will realize what
amazing things he does.
PSALM 64:9 TLB

❖

You are great, and do great miracles. You alone are God.
PSALM 86:10 TLB

❖

You are the God of miracles and wonders!
You still demonstrate your awesome power.
PSALM 77:14 TLB

❖

LORD God of Israel,
we praise you.
Only you can work miracles.
PSALM 72:18 CEV

. . . I will pray.

Dear Lord,

When I was very small, I believed in everything: Santa Claus, the Easter Bunny, the Tooth Fairy, and Spiderman. When I got a little older, I went through a phase where I believed in hardly anything, especially anything that my parents believed in. But here I am, needing something that no fairy-tale character could possibly provide. I need a miracle.

Not everyone believes in miracles. In fact, I wasn't sure I did, until I realized that it is the only hope for the situation I'm in. I need something that only You can handle. It is something only You can understand. In fact, it is something only You would care about.

Lord, help me believe that You can do something about this. Help me look for Your answer to this prayer in ways that I might not have expected. Help me to resist the temptation to tell You how this miracle should happen and to trust that You know better than I. Help me to trust You to respond because of who You are—the Miracle-Worker.

Amen.

A miracle is an event beyond the power of any known physical law to produce; it is a spiritual occurrence produced by the power of God, a marvel, a wonder.

Billy Graham

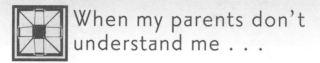

When my parents don't understand me . . .

Don't let anyone think less of you because you are young. Be an example to all believers in what you teach, in the way you live, in your love, your faith, and your purity.

1 TIMOTHY 4:12 NLT

❖

Children, obey your parents in the Lord [as His representatives], for this is just and right. Honor (esteem and value as precious) your father and your mother—this is the first commandment with a promise—that all may be well with you and that you may live long on the earth.

EPHESIANS 6:1-3 AMP

❖

Listen, children, to a father's instruction, and be attentive, that you may gain insight.

PROVERBS 4:1 NRSV

❖

The king's heart is like a stream of water directed by the LORD; he turns it wherever he pleases.

PROVERBS 21:1 NLT

. . . I will pray.

Heavenly Father,

I think my parents have forgotten what it's like to be young. They have had a lapse of memory about how important it is at my age that your friends think you're cool, how embarrassing it is to have to hang out with them, and how every teenager needs to figure out for himself what he believes in.

Why can't they understand what it's like to be me?

Lord, don't get me wrong. I love my parents, and I respect them too. But I don't try to tell them how to run their lives, and I think they should show me the same consideration.

I guess, if the truth were known, You probably relate to the way they feel, at times. You probably wish that all of us—young and old—would listen to You more than we do. Help me to keep that in mind and try to listen better. I know they just want what's best for me. But help them, too, Lord, to be more open to what I have to say. And help me say things in the right way so that they can hear me better.

Amen.

Understanding is a two-way street—one has to do with what you say, the other with what others say to you.

Andrea Garney

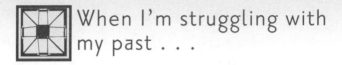

When I'm struggling with my past . . .

Forget the former things;
do not dwell on the past.
See, I am doing a new thing!
Now it springs up; do you not perceive it?
I am making a way in the desert
and streams in the wasteland.
ISAIAH 43:18-19

Throw off your old evil nature and your former way of life,
which is rotten through and through, full of lust and
deception. Instead, there must be a spiritual renewal of your
thoughts and attitudes. You must display a new nature
because you are a new person, created in God's likeness—
righteous, holy, and true.
EPHESIANS 4:22-24 NLT

Surely you know that the people who do wrong will not
receive God's kingdom. . . . In the past, some of you were like
that, but you were washed clean. You were made holy,
and you were made right with God in the name of
the Lord Jesus Christ.
1 CORINTHIANS 6:9, 11 NCV

. . . I will pray.

Dear Lord,

Late at night, when everything stops, the house gets quiet, and I end up alone, I have time to think. That's when the ghosts of the past come to pay me a visit. Make no mistake about it: they aren't friendly visitors. They haunt me with reminders of the things I've done—the things I've tried to forget.

I've wondered, if I could roll back time and undo some of those things, would they go away? If I had only known that my actions would keep coming back to me, I think I would have used better judgment.

Lord, would You help me? Would You take my guilty past and give me a new beginning—one that is tuned to my potential for the future? Show me how I can take hold of the lessons my past has taught me while putting it behind me once and for all.

Thank You, Lord, for a life of joy and laughter and freedom and right living. Thank You for taking away the old and bringing the new.

Amen.

In Christ we can move out of our past into a meaningful present and a breathtaking future.

Erwin W. Lutzer

When I need patience . . .

*We have proved ourselves to be what we claim by our
wholesome lives and by our understanding of the Gospel and
by our patience.*

2 CORINTHIANS 6:6 TLB

*We also pray that you will be strengthened with
his glorious power so that you will have all the patience
and endurance you need.*

COLOSSIANS 1:11 NLT

*We continue to shout our praise even when we're hemmed in
with troubles, because we know how troubles can develop
passionate patience in us, and how that patience in turn
forges the tempered steel of virtue, keeping us alert for
whatever God will do next.*

ROMANS 5:3-4 MSG

*See how the farmer waits for the precious fruit of the earth,
waiting patiently for it until it receives the early and latter
rain. You also be patient.*

JAMES 5:7-8 NKJV

. . . I will pray.

Heavenly Father,

I've always considered myself a pretty patient person. I don't fly off the handle over every little thing or kick the dog when things don't go my way like some people I know. But there are times when the pressure builds inside, and for one reason or another, I spew all over someone who doesn't really deserve it.

In fact, I think I'm about at the boiling point right now.

I hope You understand what I mean. I'm sure You must, because You made me, but I know it isn't how You want me to be. There is something I need to learn in this; something about how to cope with things and still treat people as I should, the way You would treat them.

Lord, give me a patient heart—and make it quick! Just kidding. Help me to develop a heart like Yours, filled with love and kindness, thinking about the other person instead of myself, and being a blessing rather than impatient and self-centered. It's what I really want—to be more like You. I love You, Lord.

Amen.

Patience is bitter, but its fruit is sweet.

Jean-Jacques Rousseau

When I need peace . . .

Embrace peace—don't let it get away!
PSALM 34:14 MSG

Happy are those who find wisdom,
and those who get understanding.
Her ways are ways of pleasantness,
and all her paths are peace.
PROVERBS 3:13, 17 NRSV

I will listen to what God the LORD will say;
he promises peace to his people, his saints.
PSALM 85:8

To all of you that are in Christ Jesus (the Messiah), may
there be peace (every kind of peace and blessing, especially
peace with God, and freedom from fears, agitating passions,
and moral conflicts).
1 PETER 5:14 AMP

. . . I will pray.

My Lord,

One minute I think I'm at peace, and the next minute, I'm totally frazzled. What's the deal? I waver between being content and being restless all the time. It isn't just a daily struggle either, Lord. It is a minute-by-minute dilemma. I really need Your help.

If I listen to what I see on television, peace comes from nations getting along and controversy being stilled. Maybe that's what makes my kind of peace so erratic. It keeps changing with the headlines. Some of my friends think peace comes from having everything you want or need. But I really doubt that would work either.

Help me find the kind of peace that fills me up on the inside and never leaves me, even during the tumultuous parts of life. I know in my heart that peace like that comes only from You—the Prince of Peace. So . . . I'm asking, Lord, and waiting for Your answer. I'm waiting, ready to lay my life at Your feet, ready to follow You wherever You may lead me. Your peace is worth going after at any price.

Amen.

All his glory and beauty come from within,
and there he delights to dwell, his visits there are
frequent, his conversations sweet, his comforts
refreshing, and his peace passing all understanding.

Thomas à Kempis

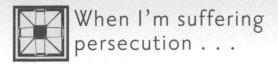# When I'm suffering persecution . . .

Everyone who wants to live a godly life in
Christ Jesus will suffer persecution.
2 TIMOTHY 3:12 NLT

Who shall separate us from the love of Christ?
Shall trouble or hardship or persecution or famine or
nakedness or danger or sword?
ROMANS 8:35

❖

[Jesus said] Remember the word that I said to you,
"A servant is not greater than his master." If they persecuted
me, they will persecute you.
JOHN 15:20 RSV

❖

[Jesus said] Love your enemies, bless them that curse you,
do good to them that hate you, and pray for them which
despitefully use you, and persecute you.
MATTHEW 5:44 KJV

. . . I will pray.

Dear Lord,

I've been having a tough time lately. Some kids have been hassling me just because I'm a Christian. I know You know how it feels, considering what You went through at the Crucifixion—I saw the movie. But is it really necessary for me to go through these things considering that I'm not in the business of saving people? I'm just trying to live my life.

The only thing I can remember from the Bible about how You handled persecution were Your words: "Father, forgive them." It doesn't even make sense to me that You cared. You obviously thought that they didn't know what they were doing.

Is it possible that is true in my case? Perhaps my peers don't realize that they are just showing their ignorance, their insecurity about what they believe—or should I say, what they don't believe. Help me, Lord, to understand where all their anger and hostility are coming from, so I'll be able to respond in the right way.

Even when it's hard, Lord, help me to walk each day in love and forgiveness the way You did.

Amen.

The servant of Christ must never be surprised if he has to drink of the same cup with his Lord.

J. C. Ryle

When I'm seeking ways to reach my potential . . .

I don't mean to say I am perfect. . . . I am still not all I should be but I am bringing all my energies to bear on this one thing: Forgetting the past and looking forward to what lies ahead, I strain to reach the end of the race and receive the prize for which God is calling us up to heaven because of what Christ Jesus did for us.

PHILIPPIANS 3:12-14 TLB

*May he give you what you want
and make all your plans succeed,
and we will shout for joy when you succeed,
and we will raise a flag in the name of our God.*

PSALM 20:4-5 NCV

*In everything you do, put God first, and he will direct you
and crown your efforts with success.*

PROVERBS 3:6 TLB

*Commit to the LORD whatever you do,
and your plans will succeed.*

PROVERBS 16:3

. . . I will pray.

Father God,

I wish I knew as much about myself as You do. I just want to know what I'm supposed to do with my life. When I was very young, I had huge plans about what I would become—a professional athlete, a rock star, or maybe even a billionaire.

These days, I'm being a little more realistic. I'm thinking a really good teacher or coach, a CEO, or a Navy Seal. I haven't really decided. But that's why I wish I knew all that You know. I don't want to waste my time. I don't want to worry about understanding Shakespeare if I'm going to be using calculus instead.

Could You help me, Lord? Please give me some direction— send someone I trust to talk to me, or give me a feeling inside, or You can even send an angel if You prefer. Any way you choose, I can take steps to begin realizing my potential. I just want to be all You planned for me to be, and I feel certain that You will help me find out what that is. Thank You, Lord, for filling me with potential and giving me a bright future.

Amen.

The potential for greatness lies in all of us.

Wilma Rudolph

When I need protection . . .

[God] orders his angels to protect you wherever you go.
PSALM 91:11 TLB

❖

You protect me with salvation-armor;
you hold me up with a firm hand,
caress me with your gentle ways.
PSALM 18:35 MSG

❖

The LORD is my light and the one who saves me.
I fear no one. The LORD protects my life;
I am afraid of no one.
PSALM 27:1 NCV

❖

GOD'S angel sets up a circle
of protection around us while we pray.
PSALM 34:7 MSG

❖

He will not let your foot slip—
he who watches over you will not slumber;
indeed, he who watches over Israel
will neither slumber nor sleep.
PSALM 121:3-4

. . . I will pray.

Dear Lord,

There are times when fear stalks me like a hungry lion and I just want to run for shelter—hiding until the roaring inside of me subsides. At times like that, I just need to feel Your protection.

For instance, when I feel like I'm about to give in to peer pressure—do something I know I'll regret—I need Your strength to say no. When I feel vulnerable to harm—the object of someone's envy, hatred, or greed—I need the reassurance that You are nearby. When I'm feeling the pressure to perform, I need your confidence to get me through. And most of all, I need the safety net of Your grace when I have fallen flat on my face—when I just can't forgive myself and can't forgive anyone else, either.

I guess I simply want to know that You are there for me no matter what—like a daddy watching over his kid—because I know that the devil is alive and well. They say he really is like a lion prowling about, trying to catch people in moments of weakness so that he can attack and destroy.

Thank You, Lord, for the shelter of Your love and protection.

Amen.

The center of God's will is our only safety.

Betsie ten Boom

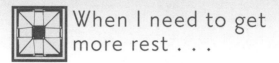# When I need to get more rest . . .

[The Lord] lets me rest in green pastures.
He leads me to calm water.
He gives me new strength.
PSALM 23:2-3 NCV

❖

On the seventh day God finished his work
which he had done, and he rested.
GENESIS 2:2 RSV

❖

[The Lord said] You must work for six days,
but on the seventh day you must rest—even during the
planting season and the harvest season.
EXODUS 34:21 NCV

❖

[Jesus said] Come to me, all you who are weary and
burdened, and I will give you rest. Take my yoke upon you
and learn from me, for I am gentle and humble in heart,
and you will find rest for your souls. For my yoke is easy
and my burden is light.
MATTHEW 11:28-30

. . . I will pray.

Father in Heaven,

Lately I haven't been at my best. I feel frazzled and strung out most of the time. It seems that there are so many things required of me and so many activities that I want to be part of that I end up not doing anything well. I really need some rest.

The problem is, when I'm not busy, I feel out of touch and even a little insecure about the world going on without me. That makes it difficult to stop the activity; turn down the noise; switch off the phones, computers, and television; and get still and quiet long enough to really rest.

It seems like I've been fighting the need to rest all my life. I'm told that even when I was a baby I fought to stay awake. I guess I'm still doing that—but I know that rest is more than just Your gift; it's Your command. So help me let go and trust that the world won't fall apart while I get a few z's.

Thank You, Lord, for putting rest in Your plan for me. Now teach me to respect and honor Your goodness every day and every night of my life.

Amen.

Renewal and restoration are not luxuries.
They are essentials. Being alone and resting for a while is not selfish. It is Christlike.

Charles R. Swindoll

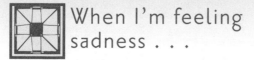# When I'm feeling sadness . . .

You changed my sorrow into dancing.
You took away my clothes of sadness,
and clothed me in happiness.

PSALM 30:11 NCV

❖

Be kind to me, GOD. . . .
I've cried my eyes out;
I feel hollow inside. . . .
Warm me, your servant, with a smile;
save me because you love me.

PSALM 31:9, 16 MSG

❖

The ransomed of the LORD will return.
They will enter Zion with singing;
everlasting joy will crown their heads.
Gladness and joy will overtake them,
and sorrow and sighing will flee away.

ISAIAH 35:10

❖

My soul is weary with sorrow;
strengthen me according to your word.

PSALM 119:28

. . . I will pray.

Dear Lord,

Sometimes, no matter how much there is to be happy about, a feeling of sadness overtakes my heart, and I can't seem to shake it off. At times, the sadness is related to circumstances, like when I get disappointed by someone, feel I've failed, or had some other discouraging situation in my life. But the worst is when I feel sad for no reason—something inside just doesn't seem right.

I read in the Bible that Jesus came to bring us joy. That's what the angels sang, isn't it—"Joy to the World"? And yet, He sure had a lot of sadness in His life too.

Lord, if You could help me get to the root of my sadness, perhaps it would help me make some needed adjustments in my perspective or perhaps in my behavior. Maybe I just need to open up more of my heart to You. I'm willing to do whatever it takes to get rid of this dark cloud that's hanging over me.

Thank You, Lord, for seeing through all the superficial stuff and helping me right where I need it. I know I can always count on You.

Amen.

No one needs to be downcast, for Jesus is the joy of heaven, and it is his joy to enter into sorrowful hearts.

Frederick William Faber

When I'm trying to balance a busy schedule . . .

Jesus replied: "'Love the Lord your God with all your heart and with all your soul and with all your mind.' This is the first and greatest commandment. And the second is like it: 'Love your neighbor as yourself.'"

MATTHEW 22:37-39

[Jesus said] Are you tired? Worn out? Burned out on religion? Come to me. Get away with me and you'll recover your life. I'll show you how to take a real rest. Walk with me and work with me—watch how I do it. Learn the unforced rhythms of grace. I won't lay anything heavy or ill-fitting on you. Keep company with me and you'll learn to live freely and lightly.

MATTHEW 11:28-30 MSG

Moses' father-in-law said, "This is no way to go about it. You'll burn out, and the people right along with you. This is way too much for you—you can't do this alone. Now listen to me. Let me tell you how to do this so that God will be in this with you."

EXODUS 18:17-19 MSG

. . . I will pray.

Father in Heaven,

I admit it, being busy makes me feel needed and important. I guess that's why I like to live my life this way. But I also have to admit that my schedule sometimes gets a little too full—even for me! I get worried that I might start dropping balls all over the place or overlook someone who's much more important than anything I might be doing.

The other thing is that when I get too busy, I don't handle interruptions very well. I tend to ignore people or get irritable. Later, when I think back on my day, I realize that all of my activity is pointless if I mistreat the people in my life.

I've read in the Bible about how busy Jesus was when He was here on earth—teaching about God and His kingdom, performing miracles, healing the sick. His mission was the most demanding ever! Yet He seemed so cool about everything, and He never ignored anyone.

So, Lord, in the midst of my busy life, I need help balancing my busy schedule. Show me how to make sure that I don't neglect the really important stuff—like the people all around me. And even more important, help to make sure that I never neglect my relationship with You.

Amen.

There is absolutely nothing enviable or spiritual about a coronary or a nervous breakdown, nor is an ultrabusy schedule necessarily the mark of a productive life.

Charles R. Swindoll

When I'm having trouble in school . . .

[God said] Haven't I commanded you? Strength!
Courage! Don't be timid; don't get discouraged. God,
your God, is with you every step you take.

JOSHUA 1:9 MSG

❖

David continued to address Solomon: "Take charge! Take
heart! Don't be anxious or get discouraged. GOD, my God, is
with you in this; he won't walk off and leave you in the lurch.
He's at your side until every last detail is completed."

1 CHRONICLES 28:20 MSG

❖

Let all who are discouraged take heart.
Come, let us tell of the LORD'S greatness; . . .
I prayed to the LORD, and he answered me,
freeing me from all my fears.

PSALM 34:2-4 NLT

❖

The LORD himself goes before you and will be with you;
he will never leave you nor forsake you. Do not be afraid;
do not be discouraged.

DEUTERONOMY 31:8

. . . I will pray.

Dear Lord,

I hate school. Not all the time, but most of the time. For one thing, I don't like to get up so early in the morning, listen to boring lectures, and study a bunch of junk that I'll never need in real life. I think if my English teacher asks us to diagram one more sentence, I'm just going to scream. And who cares about the Civil War? Not me! Who cares about multiplying fractions? Not me! School is just a big waste of time.

The truth is it isn't school I don't like—that's just kind of the front I use to cover up how bad I am at everything. Multiplying those fractions, for one—I just can't seem to figure out how to do it. If I ask questions, my friends look at me like I'm stupid or something. I feel like I'm paddling upstream—rowing as hard as I can, but still losing ground.

I don't know what to do, Lord, but I guess the place to start would be to ask someone I trust for help. Show me whom I can go to. And thanks, Lord, for being there when I don't have the courage to talk to anyone else. You really are my best Friend.

Amen.

He who asks is a fool for five minutes, but he who does not ask remains a fool forever.

Chinese Proverb

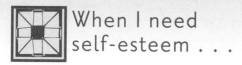

When I need self-esteem . . .

God created people in his own image.
GENESIS 1:27 NLT

❖

*[The Lord says] I have engraved you on
the palms of my hands.*
ISAIAH 49:16

❖

*[Jesus said] What's the price of a pet canary? Some loose
change, right? And God cares what happens to it even more
than you do. He pays even greater attention to you, down to
the last detail—even numbering the hairs on your head! So
don't be intimidated by all this bully talk. You're worth
more than a million canaries.*
MATTHEW 10:29-31 MSG

❖

*Oh yes, you shaped me first inside, then out;
you formed me in my mother's womb.
I thank you, High God—you're breathtaking!
Body and soul, I am marvelously made!
I worship in adoration—what a creation!*
PSALM 139:13-14 MSG

. . . I will pray.

My Lord,

Just about the time I think I have something going for myself, I blow it. I do or say something stupid and I know people are laughing behind my back, thinking that I'm such a loser. Why wouldn't they think that? I do!

This is my world. I struggle in math, but I end up seated next to the class "brain-child." He always has the answers, and I just sit there and look dumb. The same is true in P.E. and shop and every other subject. How is it possible that one person can be so consistently bad in everything?

And about my appearance: I know I'm not great-looking, but how did I manage to end up short with pimples and flat hair? But who cares? I never wanted to be popular anyway.

Someone told me once that You created me. Is that true? If it is, seems like I should be worth something. I doubt if You would mess up anything You make. I want to like myself, Lord. Let me see how I look to You. That might just change everything.

Amen.

A healthy self-image is seeing yourself as God sees you—no more and no less.

Josh McDowell

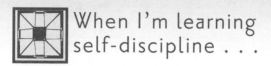

When I'm learning self-discipline . . .

God did not give us a spirit of timidity,
but a spirit of power . . . and of self-discipline.
2 TIMOTHY 1:7

❖

An undisciplined, self-willed life is puny;
an obedient, God-willed life is spacious.
PROVERBS 15:32 MSG

❖

I discipline my body and bring it into subjection, lest, when I
have preached to others, I myself should become disqualified.
1 CORINTHIANS 9:27 NKJV

❖

The Lord GOD helps me,
so I will not be ashamed.
I will be determined,
and I know I will not be disgraced.
ISAIAH 50:7 NCV

❖

All discipline for the moment seems not to be joyful,
but sorrowful; yet to those who have been trained by it,
afterwards it yields the peaceful fruit of righteousness.
HEBREWS 12:11 NASB

. . . I will pray.

Heavenly Father,

Whether it is sports, schoolwork, service projects at church, or relationships, I find it hard to discipline myself to get things done. Every aspect of life feels like a cross-country marathon to me. I start out really strong, enthused, even excited about things; but about midway through, I begin to lose interest, not to mention momentum.

How can I maintain the discipline that leads to excellence?

I've watched the high-performance people: athletes, dancers, corporate executives, doctors, entertainers, military heroes, and the like. They all have the same story to tell—how they didn't feel like getting up or practicing or focusing on their goals. But somehow they were able to rule over their feelings and stay in the game.

Bottom line, Lord, I want to know how they do it. Where do they find the self-discipline to keep going when the going gets tough? Am I capable of locking onto that inner strength I need? I hope I am, but when I'm not, I'm going to reach out to You right away in prayer. I'm going to ask for Your discipline, Your strength to get me on my feet and going again. Thank You for filling my heart with determination.

Amen.

The best discipline, maybe the only discipline that really works, is self-discipline

Walter Kiechel III

When I can't sleep . . .

The fear of the LORD leads to life,
So that one may sleep satisfied, untouched by evil.
PROVERBS 19:23 NASB

❖

Find rest, O my soul, in God alone;
my hope comes from him.
PSALM 62:5

❖

I will both lie down in peace, and sleep;
For You alone, O LORD, make me dwell in safety.
PSALM 4:8 NKJV

❖

If you sit down, you will not be afraid;
when you lie down, your sleep will be sweet.
PROVERBS 3:24 RSV

❖

The LORD gives sleep to those he loves.
PSALM 127:2 NCV

. . . I will pray.

Dear Lord,

How is it that the days fly by, but the nights—the sleepless ones, that is—stretch on forever? I toss and turn, trying to get the covers just right and find the right position for my head on my pillow, only to find that my eyelids are spring-loaded and won't stay shut.

Lord, I really need Your help on those sleepless nights. I need Your peace to still my anxious thoughts and supercharged mind. Help me to take time before I even get into bed to bow my head to You and offer You all my burdens and cares. You are the only one who can make sense of my cares anyway. If I could solve them, I wouldn't be struggling with them all night.

Thank You, Lord, for doing for me what I can't do for myself—blessing me with much-needed rest.

Amen.

Tired nature's sweet restorer, balmy sleep!

Edward Young

When I need strength . . .

The rock of my strength, my refuge is in God.
<small>PSALM 62:7 NASB</small>

Incline Your ear to me, rescue me quickly;
Be to me a rock of strength,
A stronghold to save me.
<small>PSALM 31:2 NASB</small>

❖

Those who wait on the LORD
Shall renew their strength;
They shall mount up with wings like eagles,
They shall run and not be weary,
They shall walk and not faint.
<small>ISAIAH 40:31 NKJV</small>

❖

I will boast . . . about my weaknesses, so that Christ's power
may rest on me. . . . For when I am weak, then I am strong.
<small>2 CORINTHIANS 12:9-10</small>

. . . I will pray.

Father God,

Life is hard. Not all the time, of course, but often enough that sometimes I feel weak and afraid. I don't like admitting that to my friends because it isn't cool to whine. But there are times when I need to talk to You about it, because You know all and see all, and I have the impression that You can do something about it.

What I need is strength, Lord. Some days, I need strength just to obey. I get really tired of being "good" all the time when others around me are being not-so-good. It seems like they live more exciting lives, experience more thrills, and have a lot more to boast about than I do.

Sometimes I need the strength to forgive. Every now and then, someone close to me does something really hurtful and I feel like I'm not going to get over it. I know You can help me let go and move on, learning to forgive the way You do—completely.

And there are times, Lord, when I need strength just to get through my day. Take all my weakness and put Your strength in me instead.

Amen.

When a man has no strength, if he leans on God,
he becomes powerful.

Dwight Lyman Moody

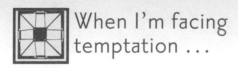

When I'm facing temptation . . .

No temptation has overtaken you except such as is common to man; but God is faithful, who will not allow you to be tempted beyond what you are able, but with the temptation will also make the way of escape, that you may be able to bear it.

1 CORINTHIANS 10:13 NKJV

❖

Blessed is anyone who endures temptation. Such a one has stood the test and will receive the crown of life that the Lord has promised to those who love him.

JAMES 1:12 NRSV

❖

[Jesus prayed] Do not lead us into temptation, but deliver us from evil.

MATTHEW 6:13 NASB

❖

[Jesus said] Keep watching and praying that you may not enter into temptation; the spirit is willing, but the flesh is weak.

MATTHEW 26:41 NASB

. . . I will pray.

Dear Lord,

Is there anyone else out there like me—anyone who struggles with the same temptations over and over again? Do You just want to give up on me? Sometimes, I wonder why You don't.

Many times, after I have fought really hard and finally won the battle, it seems like the enemy (the devil) sneaks up behind me and sets an ambush before I have time to retreat and regroup. And the worst struggles of all have to do with relationships.

The problem is, when I'm on a date—alone with someone I'm really attracted to—and having a good time, I don't think about things in terms of morality. In fact, I don't think much at all. I tend to make all of my decisions based on what I feel, as opposed to what I think.

I really need Your help with this, Lord. I've been told that You've promised to always give us a way out of temptation if we are looking for one. Help me to see Your escape route. Thank You for knowing me better than I even know myself.

Amen.

The best way to overcome temptation is to avoid the tempting situation.

Author Unknown

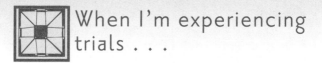

When I'm experiencing trials . . .

[The Lord] reached down from heaven and took me
and drew me out of my great trials. He rescued me
from deep waters.
PSALM 18:16 TLB

❖

Count it all joy when you fall into various trials,
knowing that the testing of your faith produces patience.
But let patience have its perfect work, that you may be perfect
and complete, lacking nothing.
JAMES 1:2-4 NKJV

❖

Beloved, do not think it strange concerning the fiery trial
which is to try you, as though some strange thing happened to
you; but rejoice to the extent that you partake of Christ's
sufferings, that when His glory is revealed, you may also be
glad with exceeding joy.
1 PETER 4:12-13 NKJV

❖

Endure trials for the sake of discipline. God is treating you
as children; for what child is there whom a parent
does not discipline?
HEBREWS 12:7 NRSV

. . . I will pray.

My Lord,

My youth minister is fond of saying that trials produce strong character. That may be true for most people, but I'm feeling a little wimpy myself. I just wish I could get a break. It's always something—my grades, friendships, issues of honesty, my health, the temptation of alcohol or drugs, and even just living day in and day out with my parents. Whatever the trials are, I seem to be plagued with them twenty-four/seven.

Why do good people have so many struggles when all we're trying to do is live right? It seems to me that it should get easier; but instead, it gets harder. My character ought to be like a solid block of steel by now for all I've gone through.

I don't mean to complain, Lord, but do You think You could maybe help me find a little breathing room? If not, could You help me learn how to cope with things a little better? I don't want to embarrass everybody, and that includes You, Lord. In fact, I don't really mind being put to the test as long as I have what I need to make it through. What I need is more of You.

Amen.

In this life we will encounter hurts and trials that we will not be able to change; we are just going to have to allow them to change us.

Ron Lee Davis

When I'm having a problem with my weight . . .

Walk in the Spirit, and you shall not fulfill the lust of the flesh. For the flesh lusts against the Spirit, and the Spirit against the flesh; and these are contrary to one another, so that you do not do the things that you wish. . . .
But the fruit of the Spirit is . . . self-control.
GALATIANS 5:16-17, 22-23 NKJV

Remember that in a race everyone runs, but only one person gets the prize. You also must run in such a way that you will win. All athletes practice strict self-control. They do it to win a prize that will fade away, but we do it for an eternal prize. So I run straight to the goal with purpose in every step. . . . I discipline my body like an athlete, training it to do what it should. Otherwise, I fear that after preaching to others I myself might be disqualified.
1 CORINTHIANS 9:24-27 NLT

❖

Those who are Christ's have crucified the flesh with its passions and desires. If we live in the Spirit, let us also walk in the Spirit.
GALATIANS 5:24-25 NKJV

. . . I will pray.

Dear Lord,

I feel fat and ugly. Every morning when I wake up, I make a promise to myself that I won't eat any donuts, fast food, potato chips, or candy bars. I won't drink any sugar-sweetened soda, either.

I'm pretty impressed with my willpower—for about one hour. Midmorning, I'm craving something chock-full of calories, and I'm running for the vending machines between classes.

It was a whole lot easier when fashion trends were oversized and baggy. Now, everything is snug and fits your body like a snakeskin. It works out great if you have no more than 2 percent body fat, but for normal people like me, the styles aren't flattering at all; they're frightening.

On top of that, I'm jealous of people whose metabolism burns food before it even hits the pits of their stomachs. They can scarf down anything they want and never gain an ounce.

Lord, can you help me find satisfaction in something other than food? I eat when I'm happy, sad, frustrated, busy, tired, mad, and bored. In other words, just about all the time. I need fulfillment that comes from the inside out, rather than having to stuff it from the outside in.

Amen.

Do not give your heart to that which does
not satisfy your heart.

Abba Poemen

When I need wisdom . . .

Without counsel, plans go awry,
But in the multitude of counselors they are established.
PROVERBS 15:22 NKJV

❖

If any of you is lacking in wisdom, ask God, who gives to all
generously and ungrudgingly, and it will be given you.
JAMES 1:5 NRSV

❖

Happy is the person who finds wisdom,
the one who gets understanding.
Wisdom is worth more than silver;
it brings more profit than gold.
Wisdom is more precious than rubies;
nothing you could want is equal to it.
With her right hand wisdom offers you a long life,
and with her left hand she gives you riches and honor.
PROVERBS 3:13-16 NCV

❖

Listen to advice and accept instruction,
and in the end you will be wise.
PROVERBS 19:20

. . . I will pray.

Heavenly Father,

About the time I think I know all I need to know, something happens to shake me up. I suppose one of the most troubling things to me is that I don't have the wisdom I need to deal with people effectively. I may think I'm doing really well, and suddenly someone gets hurt or angry, and I'm just left standing there looking shocked and stupid.

Another area where I feel I come up short on wisdom is when I have a really big decision to make. People tell me to take my time and weigh all my options. But all I can think about is the one thing that preoccupies my mind, and instead of waiting, I dive in up to my neck, unprepared to deal with the consequences of my decision. I see the wisdom of waiting—but only when it's too late.

Lord, I know You major in wisdom. I sure could use some of it. Help me slow down and see the value in seeking good advice from others. Most importantly, help me remember to take the time to talk to You before I run off and get myself in trouble.

Amen.

Knowledge is the power of the mind,
Wisdom is the power of the soul.

Julie Shannahan

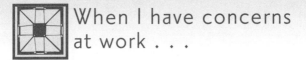

When I have concerns at work . . .

Fire goes out for lack of fuel,
and tensions disappear when gossip stops.
Proverbs 26:20 TLB

❖

My life is worth nothing unless I use it for doing the work
assigned me by the Lord Jesus.
Acts 20:24 NLT

❖

In all the work you are doing, work the best you can.
Work as if you were doing it for the Lord, not for people.
Remember that you will receive your reward from the Lord,
which he promised to his people. You are serving
the Lord Christ.
Colossians 3:23-24 NCV

❖

To enjoy your work and to accept your lot in life—
that is indeed a gift from God. The person who does that
will not need to look back with sorrow on his past,
for God gives him joy.
Ecclesiastes 5:19-20 TLB

. . . I will pray.

Dear Lord,

I suppose everyone has to deal with whacked-out stuff that goes on at work. I've heard that because every organization is made up of human beings, every ugly thing about human nature shows up in the workplace. I can sure see that!

I hate how much nasty talking goes on at times. It starts out being kind of harmless, but it grows. People's reputations get damaged, feelings get hurt, and people don't trust each other anymore. Gossip changes everything for everyone. I just wish people would think before they start waggin' their tongues.

Then there's all the unfair stuff that happens. A lot of it goes on behind the scenes. But pretty soon the schedules come out and the work assignments aren't delegated evenly. All of a sudden there are little knots of people around every corner, even in the restrooms, talking and accusing and pointing fingers. It makes me sick.

What should I do about this? Should I talk to my boss, my coworkers, or just to You? I need Your wisdom, Father, to do the right thing when wrong happens at work. I'm really glad I can count on You, Lord, for wisdom and for everything.

Amen.

When you walk with God, he walks with you—at home, at work, at school. No matter when, no matter where, call on him and he will help you.

Andrea Garney

God, be merciful to me;
On Thy grace I rest my plea;
In Thy vast, abounding grace,
My transgressions all erase.
Wash me wholly from my sin;
Cleanse from every ill within.

The Psalter

Prayers of Confession

Lifting My Voice to God
When I Need Forgiveness

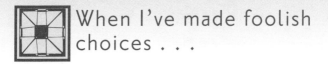

When I've made foolish choices . . .

Words kill, words give life;
they're either poison or fruit—you choose.
PROVERBS 18:21 MSG

❖

A mirror reflects a man's face, but what he is really like is
shown by the kind of friends he chooses.
PROVERBS 27:19 TLB

❖

He shows how to distinguish right from wrong, how to find
the right decision every time.
PROVERBS 2:9 TLB

❖

Who are they that fear the LORD?
He will teach them the way that they should choose.
PSALM 25:12 NRSV

❖

Choose my teachings instead of silver,
and knowledge rather than the finest gold.
PROVERBS 8:10 NCV

. . . I will pray.

Dear Lord,

I made a decision today that hurt those who love me most. I knew I was thinking only of myself; but at that moment, I didn't care. And now, I deeply regret it. I don't want to be that kind of person. I want to be wise and thoughtful as I make those daily choices. I see now that little choices can have a big impact on my relationships, my future—even my health.

The problem is that good choices always look simple when it's too late. I need to be able to choose wisely in the moment, and that's pretty hard. I really need Your help, Lord. I need to feel You strong inside me, guiding and encouraging me to do what is right.

I know that You are my Answer. My parents aren't with me all the time, but You are. I carry You with me into the middle of every conversation, every situation I face. Speak to my heart, Lord—right here on the spot. If I'm not quick to listen, give me a solid nudge. When my choices are pleasing to You, I know they will mean life and happiness for me.

Amen.

By the mercy of God we may repent a wrong choice
and alter the consequences by making a new
and right choice.

A. W. Tozer

When I've become critical an
judgmental . . .

Don't grumble about each other,
my brothers and sisters, or God will judge you.
JAMES 5:9 NLT

❖

[Jesus said] Don't pick on people, jump on their failures, criticize
their faults—unless, of course, you want the same treatment. That
critical spirit has a way of boomeranging.
MATTHEW 7:1-2 MSG

❖

The whole Law can be summed up in this one command:
"Love others as you love yourself." But if instead of showing love
among yourselves you are always critical and catty, watch out!
Beware of ruining each other.
GALATIANS 5:14-15 TLB

❖

Encourage one another and build up one another.
1 THESSALONIANS 5:11 NASB

❖

Encourage one another day after day, as long as it is
still called "Today," so that none of you will be hardened
by the deceitfulness of sin.
HEBREWS 3:13 NASB

. . . I will pray.

Heavenly Father,

I don't mean to be so judgmental when my friends share their secrets. Sometimes I feel my face tightening up into a frown without my even trying. Especially when I hear my friends tell me that they've been sleeping with their boyfriends or staying out late drinking. I want to listen and not condemn or be critical. But I'm usually tempted to lecture or, worse yet, get all self-righteous.

Still, there must be a reason why people continue to confide in me. Could it be that You've put me in their lives to help them make better choices? That's a humbling thought. I want to be worthy of that kind of trust. To give them good advice; not to judge or distance myself from them.

I need Your heart of compassion, Lord. Forgive me for being judgmental and critical. Thank You for having compassion for me when I sin. We both know I'm nowhere near perfect myself. I know, with Your help, I can also learn to be less critical and truly help my friends when they're in need.

Amen.

The faults of others are like headlights
of an approaching car—they always seem
more glaring than our own.
Author Unknown

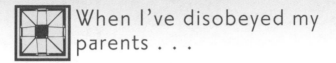

When I've disobeyed my parents . . .

*Children, obey your parents in the Lord, for this is right.
"Honor your father and mother" (this is the first
commandment with a promise), "that it may be well with you
and that you may live long on the earth."*

Ephesians 6:1-3 rsv

❖

*If you are willing and obedient,
You shall eat the good of the land.*

Isaiah 1:19 nkjv

❖

*Those who reject what they are taught will pay for it,
but those who obey what they are told will be rewarded.*

Proverbs 13:13 ncv

❖

*Children who obey what they have been taught are smart,
but friends of troublemakers disgrace their parents.*

Proverbs 28:7 ncv

. . . I will pray.

Dear Lord,

It's hard to obey my parents, sometimes—especially when a friend tempts me to do something I know I shouldn't. Whether it's staying out late, or going against the school's dress code, or even watching a horror movie (when I know my parents wouldn't want me to), these things all tempt me to disobey.

Oh, I can come up with all kinds of excuses for my disobedience (my parents are hopelessly outdated, they don't understand my generation, blah, blah, blah . . .). But, in the end, they're still my parents—and I know it's important to obey them. As my dad often says, family rules are there for my protection. And there are consequences when I disobey—like feeling isolated from my parents. I love them and want us to feel close.

Please forgive me for my disobedience. I need help, Lord, to stand up against the temptations around me—the things that whisper that it's okay to disobey. Thank You for giving me parents who love me and are concerned for me. And thank You that You've promised to bless me with good things when I obey them.

Amen.

The cost of obedience is small compared to
the cost of disobedience.

Author Unknown

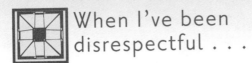

When I've been disrespectful . . .

Be submissive to your masters with all respect,
not only to those who are good and gentle, but also to
those who are unreasonable.

1 PETER 2:18 NASB

❖

Show respect for everyone. Love your Christian brothers and
sisters. Fear God. Show respect for the king.

1 PETER 2:17 NLT

❖

Give everyone what you owe him: If you owe taxes, pay
taxes; . . . if respect, then respect; if honor, then honor.

ROMANS 13:7

❖

Honor those leaders who work so hard for you,
who have been given the responsibility of urging and guiding
you along in your obedience. Overwhelm them with
appreciation and love!

1 THESSALONIANS 5:12-13 MSG

❖

. . . I will pray.

My Father in Heaven,

I try to be respectful of others—especially people who are older than I am. But sometimes it's hard. How can I show respect for people I don't like? Some people can be so unreasonable. Like my boss, when he asks me to work overtime (and on a holiday weekend too!). Who wouldn't be upset about something like that?

Oh, I know the little signs of disrespect need to go. When I roll my eyes or snicker at a teacher or my boss, I know that doesn't please You, Lord. I know You've put those people in authority over me for a reason, and that I need to respect them—even when they ask me to do something that seems unfair.

I'm sorry I've been disrespectful. I know, Lord, that with Your help I can "lose the 'tude" and become genuinely respectful of others. I'll work really hard on getting rid of the eye rolling and the rude comments. Thank You that You'll give me the self-control I need to be found trustworthy in this area, and that my teachers, parents, and yes, even my bosses will have full confidence in me.

Amen.

Respect is love in plain clothes.

Frankie Byrne

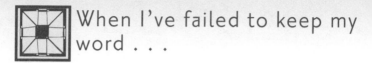

When I've failed to keep my word . . .

Keep your word even when it costs you.
PSALM 15:4 MSG

❖

O God, . . . help me never to tell a lie.
PROVERBS 30:7-8 TLB

❖

*[The Lord commanded] If a man makes a promise to the
LORD or says he will do something special, he must keep his
promise. He must do what he said.*
NUMBERS 30:2 NCV

❖

*If you do not make the promise, you will not be guilty. You
must do whatever you say you will do, because you chose to
make the promise to the LORD your God.*
DEUTERONOMY 23:22-23 NCV

❖

*He stores up sound wisdom for the upright;
He is a shield to those who walk in integrity.*
PROVERBS 2:7 NASB

. . . I will pray.

Dear Lord,

I've always prided myself on being a person of my word. Someone who keeps her promises, no matter what the circumstances. Someone who can always be counted on, day or night, rain or shine. But I just blew it; I didn't keep my word. And I feel awful about it.

I didn't mean to let this person down. I really did have good intentions. But my own selfish desires got in the way. And the honest truth is, in the end, I did what I wanted to do. And, in the process, I lost this person's trust. Now, I need to find a way to show this person how sorry I am.

I guess what I'm asking for is a second chance to honor You, Lord, by being faithful, true, and trustworthy. I'm so glad You love me enough to give me that chance. Please give this other person grace to forgive me and give me a second chance, as well. With Your help, Lord, I know I can become a person whose word others can depend on.

Amen.

He who is slow in making a promise is most likely to be faithful in the performance of it.

Jean-Jacques Rousseau

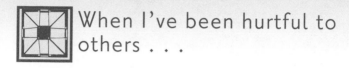# When I've been hurtful to others . . .

Put these things out of your life: anger, bad temper, doing or saying things to hurt others, and using evil words when you talk. Do not lie to each other. You have left your old sinful life and the things you did before. You have begun to live the new life, in which you are being made new and are becoming like the One who made you.

COLOSSIANS 3:8-10 NCV

The tongue runs wild, a wanton killer. With our tongues we bless God our Father; with the same tongues we curse the very men and women he made in his image.
Curses and blessings out of the same mouth! My friends, this can't go on. A spring doesn't gush fresh water one day and brackish the next, does it?

JAMES 3:8-11 MSG

[Jesus said] When you are offering your gift at the altar, if you remember that your brother or sister has something against you, leave your gift there before the altar and go; first be reconciled to your brother or sister, and then come and offer your gift.

MATTHEW 5:23-24 NRSV

. . . I will pray.

My Lord,

I have a lot of freedoms in my life. I get to go to different places and hang out with my friends. Overall, life is good. So why do I lash out sometimes and hurt others? I don't know what makes me act that way.

It takes so little to wound others: a sarcastic comment, a hurtful word. I see their sad looks and know it cuts them deep inside. That's painful to realize. I don't want to be a hurtful person, Lord. I want to show love and respect for the people in my life.

I'm sorry, Lord. I know the way I've acted is hurtful to others and to You as well. You gave me my friends and family and put love in their hearts for me. Now I want to appreciate that more and show that appreciation through my actions. I want to mirror that love back to them. Forgive me, Lord, and show me how to do better. Help me to tame my tongue, so those little comments won't slip out anymore.

Thank You that You can make me into a person others can trust to never wound them—a person who always works to build others up.

Amen.

Cold words freeze people, and hot words scorch them, and bitter words make them bitter, and wrathful words make them wrathful. Kind words . . . soothe, and quiet, and comfort the hearer.

Blaise Pascal

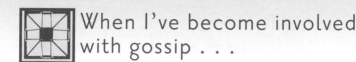

When I've become involved with gossip . . .

A gossip goes about telling secrets,
but one who is trustworthy in spirit keeps a confidence.
PROVERBS 11:13 NRSV

❖

Mean people spread mean gossip;
their words smart and burn.
Troublemakers start fights;
gossips break up friendships.
PROVERBS 16:27-28 MSG

❖

Evil people relish malicious conversation;
the ears of liars itch for dirty gossip.
PROVERBS 17:4 MSG

❖

Though some tongues just love the taste of gossip, Christians
have better uses for language than that.
EPHESIANS 5:4 MSG

. . . I will pray.

Heavenly Father,

I want to be a kind person—someone others can trust. So why is it, every time I'm around this certain group of friends, I start gossiping? Oh, it may be about stupid, silly things—the new girl's outfit, the substitute teacher's weird hairpiece, who dumped whom to go out with someone else—but it's so easy to let things slip out. And once they're out, I usually wish I could stuff them back in.

I know that gossiping really breaks down trust between people—I mean, how likely am I to trust this group with my secrets? Not very! And it can hurt, too, especially when the person being gossiped about overhears our comments. I feel like digging a hole and just climbing in when that happens.

Please forgive me, for getting caught up in gossip. I know You can help me, Lord, to regain people's trust. That You will help me to control what I say, if I'm willing. Thank You that You can give me self-control to rein in my tongue, and that You'll give me words of kindness that will lift people up.

Amen.

Never believe anything bad about anybody unless
you positively know it to be true; never tell even that
unless you feel that it is absolutely necessary—and
remember that God is listening while you tell it.

Henry Van Dyke

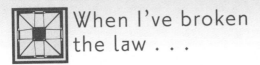

When I've broken the law . . .

*For the Lord's sake, obey every law of your government:
those of the king as head of the state, and those of the king's
officers, for he has sent them to punish all who do wrong,
and to honor those who do right.*

1 PETER 2:13-14 TLB

❖

*Obey your leaders and submit to them, for they keep watch
over your souls as those who will give an account.*

HEBREWS 13:17 NASB

❖

*Remind the people to respect the government and be
law-abiding, always ready to lend a helping hand.*

TITUS 3:1 MSG

❖

*I've tried everything and nothing helps.
I'm at the end of my rope. Is there no one who can do
anything for me? Isn't that the real question? The answer,
thank God, is that Jesus Christ can and does. He acted to set
things right in this life of contradictions where I want to serve
God with all my heart and mind, but am pulled by the
influence of sin to do something totally different.*

ROMANS 7:24-25 MSG

. . . I will pray.

Dear Lord,

I'm not sure exactly why, but when I see a sign posted saying, "Do Not . . .", well, I just want to do it. "Do Not Spit" starts my mouth salivating. "Do Not Run," and I'm itching to throw my shoes off and take off running. Even the "Slow: School Crossing" signs don't slow me down much. If anything, they make me want to speed up.

I know we have rules for a reason. And it worries me sometimes that I'm so tempted to disobey them. I feel that this impulsiveness in me could really destroy my life if I allow it to go unchallenged.

So I need Your help, Lord, to obey those laws—even the ones that seem silly. I know You can help me grow in obedience in this area. Thank You for the hope that one day I won't even have that "itch" to break those laws anymore—at the very least, I'll have the willpower not to scratch it!

Amen.

The law orders; grace supplies the power of acting.

Saint Augustine of Hippo

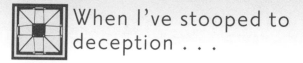

When I've stooped to deception . . .

What this adds up to, then, is this: no more lies, no more pretense. Tell your neighbor the truth. In Christ's body we're all connected to each other, after all. When you lie to others, you end up lying to yourself.

EPHESIANS 4:25 MSG

❖

[Jesus said] He [the devil] is a liar and the father of lies. But . . . I tell the truth.

JOHN 8:44-45 NRSV

❖

Keep deception and lies far from me.

PROVERBS 30:8 NASB

❖

Listen to me! For I have important information for you. Everything I say is right and true, for I hate lies and every kind of deception.

PROVERBS 8:6-7 TLB

❖

He who speaks the truth gives honest evidence, but a false witness utters deceit.

PROVERBS 12:17 RSV

. . . I will pray.

My Father,

Sometimes lying just seems the easy way out. Being honest can be tough—especially when it's about something I've done wrong. Would it really hurt someone if I told a "little white lie"? Only problem is, there's really nothing "white" about a lie—or "little" either. I don't feel particularly white—clean—inside when I lie. And those little lies have a way of turning into big ones pretty quickly.

I fool myself into thinking that "half-lies" aren't so bad, some days. I pretend that telling my parents I'm all done with my homework—when I'm mostly done—is all right. After all, I can always finish it up later—after the movie, the trip to the mall— right? Only problem is, I usually don't. And when my parents find out I wasn't finished after all, they feel that they can't trust me. And I want to be trustworthy. To be honest in everything I do or say.

And with Your help, Lord, I will be. I'm sorry for being dishonest. You delight in me when I'm truthful; and I know that You'll help me become a person others can trust.

Amen.

The essence of lying is in deception, not in words;
a lie may be told by silence, by equivocation, by the
accent on a syllable, by a glance of the eye attaching a
peculiar significance to a sentence.

John Ruskin

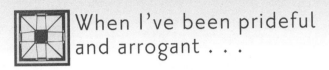

When I've been prideful and arrogant . . .

Pride will ruin people,
but those who are humble will be honored.

PROVERBS 29:23 NCV

❖

Love is . . . not arrogant or rude.

1 CORINTHIANS 13:4-5 RSV

❖

Talk no more so very proudly,
let not arrogance come from your mouth.

1 SAMUEL 2:3 NRSV

❖

Pride goes before destruction and haughtiness before a fall.

PROVERBS 16:18 TLB

❖

What makes you better than anyone else? What do you have
that God hasn't given you? And if all you have is from God,
why boast as though you have accomplished
something on your own?

1 CORINTHIANS 4:7 NLT

. . . I will pray.

Dear Lord,

I don't mean to be prideful when someone praises me for something I have done well. I wish I could just smile politely and shrug it off modestly. But, boy, do I like to hear those compliments—and not only from my parents. I mean, they're not really objective, anyway. When a teacher or another adult tells me what a good job I did—on a test, at an audition, at a rehearsal—it just seems even sweeter.

I know we're supposed to love ourselves, that it's healthy to have a good self-image. But I have this nagging feeling that I go overboard sometimes. That maybe I love myself just a little too much. That I step on others to get to the top. And then, that healthy love begins to sour.

Lord, forgive me for being prideful about my accomplishments. You've given me those abilities to glorify You, not myself. Help me never to lose sight of that. Thank You for giving each of us our own unique talents, and for helping us to use them to bless others too.

Amen.

Pride is the ground in which all the other sins grow, and the parent from which all the other sins come.

William Barclay

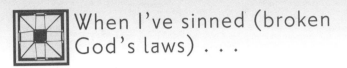# When I've sinned (broken God's laws) . . .

If we admit our sins—make a clean breast of them—[God]
won't let us down; he'll be true to himself. He'll forgive our
sins and purge us of all wrongdoing.
1 JOHN 1:9 MSG

❖

Your word I have hidden in my heart,
That I might not sin against You.
PSALM 119:11 NKJV

❖

Blessed are those whose iniquities are forgiven,
and whose sins are covered;
blessed is the one against whom the Lord will not reckon sin.
ROMANS 4:7-8 NRSV

❖

Keep your servant also from willful sins;
may they not rule over me.
Then will I be blameless,
innocent of great transgression.
PSALM 19:13

. . . I will pray.

My Lord,

Sometimes, as the apostle Paul said, "The things I don't want to do, I do." I can totally relate! I'm having a tough time right now with keeping my dating relationships pure. Things start out all right, but before long my thoughts start to take me in the wrong direction.

My friends tease me and say, "Everybody's doing it!" But even if that's true, that doesn't make it right. The guilt I feel the next day tells me that. And when I try to fool myself into thinking that making out will draw my date and me closer, deep down I know better—it always ends up tearing us apart. The way we avoid looking at each other the next day is sure proof of that.

Lord, forgive me for doing things I know are wrong. Thank You that You've promised You'll give me self-control when I ask for Your help in these situations. Thank You that, every time I resist sin, I'll get stronger in that area; and the next time temptation pops up, it won't be nearly so irresistible.

Amen.

Christ's death on the cross included a sacrifice for all our sins, past, present, and future. Every sin that you will ever commit has already been paid for.

Erwin W. Lutzer

When I've neglected my responsibilities . . .

Don't try to avoid responsibility by saying you didn't know about it. For God knows all hearts, and he sees you.

<small>PROVERBS 24:12 NLT</small>

❖

Each person should judge his own actions and not compare himself with others. Then he can be proud for what he himself has done. Each person must be responsible for himself.

<small>GALATIANS 6:4-5 NCV</small>

❖

If God has given you leadership ability, take the responsibility seriously.

<small>ROMANS 12:8 NLT</small>

❖

Be very careful, then, how you live—not as unwise but as wise, making the most of every opportunity, because the days are evil.

<small>EPHESIANS 5:15-16</small>

❖

[Jesus said] Well done, good and faithful servant; you have been faithful over a little, I will set you over much; enter into the joy of your master.

<small>MATTHEW 25:21 RSV</small>

. . . I will pray.

Father in Heaven,

I want to be responsible—I really do. It's just hard, sometimes, when other things are calling my name. Tempting me to "come out and play." Then, that fish tank suddenly doesn't look quite so murky, after all (maybe it doesn't need to be cleaned today . . .). Or the dishes don't really have to be done right away, do they? It feels like a tug-of-war inside of me some days.

Deep down, I do want to do what's right and be reliable. And I guess that's the part You see, Lord—the responsible kid lurking underneath the "I'll do it later" exterior. Maybe that's what my parents see also. Maybe that's why they never seem to give up on me, even when I blow it and don't do the things I've promised I'll do.

Forgive me for neglecting my responsibilities. Help me to become that person inside of me, Lord—the one who is responsible and can be counted on. Thank You for Your promise that when we're responsible with the little jobs, You'll give us even bigger jobs—and more responsibility—in the future.

Amen.

Character—the willingness to accept responsibility
for one's own life—is the source from which
self-respect springs.

Joan Didion

When I need to be in right relationship with God . . .

We can rejoice in our wonderful new relationship with God
—all because of what our Lord Jesus Christ has done for us
in making us friends of God.

ROMANS 5:11 NLT

Draw near to God and He will draw near to you.

JAMES 4:8 NKJV

Cultivate your own relationship with God.

ROMANS 14:22 MSG

Your fellowship with God enables you to gain a victory
over the Evil One.

1 JOHN 2:14 MSG

[Jesus said] Look! I have been standing at the door and
I am constantly knocking. If anyone hears me calling him
and opens the door, I will come in and fellowship with
him and he with me.

REVELATION 3:20 TLB

. . . I will pray.

Dear Lord,

I feel guilty a lot, lately—I'm not sure exactly why. Restless and discontent too. Maybe it's because I feel so far from You, God. When I go to church and the youth pastor asks how many of us have quiet times, I raise my hand like everyone else. But the truth is, I don't. My Bible sits on my bookshelf, gathering dust. And worship? It just feels shallow. Oh, I raise my hands and sing as loudly as the next person, but I feel empty. Like there's a hole inside of me.

I know it's not supposed to be like this, that You want me to feel close to You and full of peace and joy. I want to get back to that place of intimacy with You, Lord.

I'm sorry for neglecting my relationship with You. Please draw me close to You again. Thank You that even now, You're waiting, but not quietly. You're whispering to my heart, nudging my conscience, making sure that I don't forget my promise to always honor You in my life. Thanks for Your promise, Lord, that You will never let me go.

Amen.

Religion is humans trying to work their way to God through good works. Christianity is God coming to men and women through Jesus Christ offering them a relationship with himself.

Josh McDowell

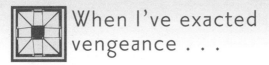

When I've exacted vengeance . . .

Love . . . is not touchy or fretful or resentful;
it takes no account of the evil done to it
[it pays no attention to a suffered wrong].
1 CORINTHIANS 13:5 AMP

❖

Don't say, "I'll pay you back for the wrong you did."
Wait for the LORD, and he will make things right.
PROVERBS 20:22 NCV

❖

Beloved, never avenge yourselves, but leave room for the
wrath of God; for it is written, "Vengeance is mine, I will
repay, says the Lord." No, "if your enemies are hungry, feed
them; if they are thirsty, give them something to drink; for by
doing this you will heap burning coals on their heads." Do not
be overcome by evil, but overcome evil with good.
ROMANS 12:19-21 NRSV

❖

Do not seek revenge or bear a grudge against one of your
people, but love your neighbor as yourself. I am the LORD.
LEVITICUS 19:18

. . . I will pray.

My Father,

Sometimes it makes me so mad, the stupid things people do. The mean things. Like breaking up with their boyfriend or girlfriend the week before Valentine's Day. Or keying another person's new car—and then laughing about it with their friends. That kind of thing makes me so angry. I just want to lash out at them. Maybe key their car, in return.

But I know that trying to take revenge on someone just ends up making me feel miserable. Worse, even, than before. Oh, there might be some immediate satisfaction in it. But that feeling fades quickly, and I'm left just feeling awful, as if I've sunk to their level. And then everything in life seems kind of bleak.

Lord, I know You want me to let go of my anger and let You handle things. You've promised that You'll bring justice when someone treats me badly—that I don't need to seek revenge. Forgive me for trying to produce justice on my own. Thanks for helping me forgive people when they've been hurtful, and thanks for modeling forgiveness for me. You're the best Friend anyone ever had.

Amen.

The noblest vengeance is to forgive.
Henry George Bohn

Make me an intercessor,
One who can really pray,
One of "the Lord's remembrancers"
By night as well as day.

Author Unknown

Prayers of
Intercession

Lifting My Voice to God
on Behalf of Others

When my friend or family member is dealing with addiction . . .

[Jesus said] If the Son sets you free, you will be free indeed.
JOHN 8:36

❖

On God rests my deliverance and my honor;
my mighty rock, my refuge is God.
PSALM 62:7 RSV

❖

Sin will have no dominion over you,
since you are . . . under grace.
ROMANS 6:14 RSV

❖

[The Lord] sent from on high, He took me;
He drew me out of many waters.
He delivered me from my strong enemy,
And from those who hated me, for they were too mighty for me.
PSALM 18:16-17 NASB

❖

O Lord, you have freed me from my bonds
and I will serve you forever.
PSALM 116:16 TLB

. . . I will pray.

Dear Lord,

I get that it's sometimes impossible to stop doing something you know is bad for you. But I'm really worried about my friend—can't he see what his addiction is doing to him? It's just destroying his life, piece by piece. And it's not just his own health that's at risk here; his whole family is affected by his choices.

I don't want to come across as judgmental—we all have things that seem, at times, to be impossible to give up. So I need Your help, Lord. Give me the right words to say to him—words that will give him hope that he can beat this thing for good. And give me an extra measure of compassion for him during this time—a willingness to listen as he shares his struggles and an eagerness to pray for him. Give him the courage to seek out the help he needs.

Thank You that You can give us the power to conquer our addictions; that we don't have to be slaves to our bad habits. I know that with Your help we can all live lives of true freedom.

Amen.

Freedom is a gift from heaven.

Denis Diderot

When my friend or family member is dealing with conflict . . .

Whoever is slow to anger has great understanding,
but one who has a hasty temper exalts folly.
PROVERBS 14:29 NRSV

❖

A soft answer turns away wrath,
but a harsh word stirs up anger.
PROVERBS 15:1 NRSV

❖

Those who are hot-tempered stir up strife,
but those who are slow to anger calm contention.
PROVERBS 15:18 NRSV

❖

A fool gives full vent to anger,
but the wise quietly holds it back.
PROVERBS 29:11 NRSV

❖

Pursue peace with all people.
HEBREWS 12:14 NKJV

. . . I will pray.

Dear Lord,

Conflict's a part of life—I get that. But why does my friend have to deal with so much of it right now? It makes me sad to see him stressed out like that. I wish I could "fix" things, to make life easier for him. But I feel like there's not much I can really do. I guess that's where You come in, Lord.

Some people are harder to get along with than others, and that can be tough. But I know that You still want us to work at getting along with people—even when they're being difficult. So please help my friend, Lord, as he deals with this conflict. Help him to have self-control, so he won't lose his temper and make things worse. Give me words of encouragement for him as he faces this situation.

Thank You that You can help him rise above this conflict and will bless him with even better things in the future, as he's faithful to work at maintaining peace in all his relationships. Thank You for the hope that, even when things are tough, You're right there with us, holding our hands and encouraging us.

Amen.

Another way to get rid of an enemy is to turn him into a friend.

Author Unknown

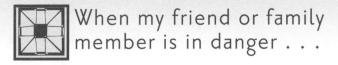

When my friend or family member is in danger . . .

God's angel sets up a circle
of protection around us while we pray.
PSALM 34:7 MSG

❖

He did deliver us from mortal danger. And we are confident
that he will continue to deliver us. He will rescue us because
you are helping by praying for us. As a result, many will give
thanks to God because so many people's prayers for
our safety have been answered.
2 CORINTHIANS 1:10-11 NLT

❖

The LORD answer you in the day of trouble!
The name of the God of Jacob protect you!
PSALM 20:1 RSV

❖

Let all who take refuge in you rejoice;
let them ever sing for joy.
Spread your protection over them.
PSALM 5:11 NRSV

. . . I will pray.

Father God,

Whenever I drive by an accident, it always hits me in the pit of my stomach: *That could be someone I know!* A lot of my friends are such crazy drivers, careening down the road at top speed and bragging that they "laugh at danger." But when I see those car wrecks, I know it's not funny.

It's strange: when you hear about people getting into accidents, it seems like it's always someone else that's affected—never someone you know. But I realize that if my friends don't start slowing down, one day it might be my phone that's ringing with bad news about some horrific accident.

I know, Lord, that You don't want me to live in fear. That Your desire is that I live a life of peace, not worried about the "what-ifs" that I have no control over. So I pray for help in releasing my fear to You. Thanks for watching over my friends and protecting them. Help them to make wiser decisions. And thanks for Your promise that You'll give me peace that surpasses anything else in life, when I hand things over to You.

Amen.

Believing God's promises the Christian is taken through difficulties of every shape and size—and arrives safely.

Richard C. Halverson

When my friend or family member goes through divorce . . .

The LORD has anointed me
To bring good news to the afflicted;
He has sent me to bind up the brokenhearted, . . .
To comfort all who mourn.

ISAIAH 61:1-2 NASB

❖

The Lord God has given me his words of wisdom so that I
may know what I should say to all these weary ones.
Morning by morning he wakens me and opens my
understanding to his will.

ISAIAH 50:4 TLB

❖

God shall wipe away all tears from their eyes.

REVELATION 7:17 KJV

❖

He is the source of every mercy and the God who comforts us.
He comforts us in all our troubles so that we can comfort
others. When others are troubled, we will be able to give them
the same comfort God has given us.

2 CORINTHIANS 1:3-4 NLT

. . . I will pray.

Dear Lord,

So many of my friends come from broken homes. Single moms, weekend dads—everyone's upset and anxious all the time. It's gotten to the point where it doesn't even surprise me anymore when I hear of another friend whose family is splitting up.

I know my friends hurt when their parents are divorcing. They might try to act cool about it, but I can see the pain in their eyes. It's tough on everyone in the family when parents split up. So I need Your compassion and tenderness at times like this, Lord. I know Your heart is breaking too.

Thank You for giving me the right words to say to my friends, Lord—words that will bring healing and hope for the future. Remind me to pray for them and to be there to listen when they are feeling frustrated and angry.

Thank You for all the times You've comforted me in the past; those times give me renewed compassion for others who are hurting. Thank You for being the God of all comfort.

Amen.

When God sees a scar, . . . he creates a star!

Robert Harold Schuller

When my friend or family member is struggling with finances . . .

I was young, and now I am old,
but I have never seen good people left helpless
or their children begging for food.

PSALM 37:25 NCV

❖

God can give you more blessings than you need. Then you
will always have plenty.

2 CORINTHIANS 9:8 NCV

❖

Even strong young lions sometimes go hungry, but those of us
who reverence the Lord will never lack any good thing.

PSALM 34:10 TLB

❖

[The Lord said]
This is my resting place forever;
here I will reside, for I have desired it.
I will abundantly bless its provisions;
I will satisfy its poor with bread.

PSALM 132:14-15 NRSV

. . . I will pray.

My Father,

Maybe I take it for granted that I'll usually have a little cash in my wallet. Our family's always had a nice house, decent cars, money for stuff we need. But I know there are lots of families who don't have "the basics." Even when some of my friends work at after-school jobs to help out, things are still tight for them financially.

I guess that's why some of them don't want to go to the mall much anymore. It's too hard to see all those cool things and not be able to buy anything. So it's just easier not to go.

I feel bad about that.

So I guess I need wisdom, Lord, to know how to help my friends. I know they don't want handouts or charity. Maybe the best thing I can do for them right now is pray for them.

Please bless their hard work, Lord, and bring in money for their families. Thank You that You've promised to take care of all of our needs and that Your desire is to open up the windows of heaven and pour out blessings on us.

Amen.

The difficulties, hardships, and trials of life,
the obstacles one encounters on the road to fortune,
are positive blessings. They knit the muscles more
firmly, and teach self-reliance.

William Mathews

When my friend or family member is experiencing grief . . .

To all who mourn in Israel he will give: beauty for ashes; joy instead of mourning; praise instead of heaviness. For God has planted them like strong and graceful oaks for his own glory.
ISAIAH 61:3 TLB

❖

He was despised and forsaken of men,
A man of sorrows and acquainted with grief; . . .
Surely our griefs He Himself bore,
And our sorrows He carried.
ISAIAH 53:3-4 NASB

❖

Blessed be the God . . . of all comfort, who comforts us in all our tribulation, that we may be able to comfort those who are in any trouble, with the comfort with which we ourselves are comforted by God.
2 CORINTHIANS 1:3-4 NKJV

❖

The Lord has comforted his people, and will have compassion upon them in their sorrow.
ISAIAH 49:13 TLB

. . . I will pray.

Father in Heaven,

What do you say to people when they've lost something precious to them? When they seem about to give up hope? My family member's in a situation like that, Lord. Her pain is almost unbearable. I need wisdom to know how to pray for her. My heart just aches with sadness.

I know You're familiar with sorrow, Lord. That You understand our pain: whether it's the pain of losing a child (after all, You did lose Your own), or a friend, or some other type of suffering that we endure. Your Son, Jesus, even wept when His own friend died. He certainly experienced pain and suffering. So even in the midst of this difficult time, I'm comforted knowing that You understand our feelings when we're grieving.

Help my family member know that same comfort, Lord. Give me words to say that aren't just clichés, but that will truly help her. Thank You that You can work miracles; that she can find renewed hope in You. You're a God of compassion, Lord. Thank You for wrapping Your arms around us when we're hurting and never letting go.

Amen.

How shall we comfort those who weep?
By weeping with them.

Father Yelchaninov

When my friend or family member needs guidance . . .

The LORD of hosts . . .
is wonderful in counsel and excellent in guidance.
ISAIAH 28:29 NKJV

❖

I will instruct you (says the Lord) and guide you
along the best pathway for your life; I will advise you
and watch your progress.
PSALM 32:8 TLB

❖

[Jesus said] When He, the Spirit of truth, has come,
He will guide you into all truth.
JOHN 16:13 NKJV

❖

The dayspring from on high hath visited us, to give light to
them that sit in darkness and in the shadow of death, to guide
our feet into the way of peace.
LUKE 1:78-79 KJV

. . . I will pray.

Dear Lord,

Sometimes the future seems a little scary. There are so many decisions to make: What job should I pursue? Whom will I marry? Should I have kids—and if so, how many? It's almost overwhelming, at times, to think of all the big decisions that lie ahead. And when my friend told me about a major decision he had to make—and quickly—I wasn't quite sure what to say to him. I didn't want to steer him in the wrong direction.

I guess I could have shared with him that he can rely on You, Lord, for guidance. That You always know which path we should take. And, if we stop and ask You for directions, You'll never steer us wrong. Help my friend to seek and follow your guidance.

I know nothing takes You by surprise or overwhelms You, Lord. That You can see far ahead, down the road before us. So thank You for the comfort that brings me; it's wonderful to know that. And thanks that You have great plans in store for my friend—and me! Better plans than we could ever even dream of.

Amen.

God has led. God will lead. God is leading!

Richard C. Halverson

When my friend or family member needs emotional healing . . .

They brought to [Jesus] all sick people who were afflicted with . . . torments, . . . and He healed them.

MATTHEW 4:24 NKJV

❖

[The Lord] turned my sorrow into joy! He took away my clothes of mourning and gave me gay and festive garments to rejoice in so that I might sing glad praises to the Lord instead of lying in silence in the grave.

PSALM 30:11-12 TLB

❖

Anxiety in the heart of man causes depression, But a good word makes it glad.

PROVERBS 12:25 NKJV

❖

Floods of sorrow pour upon me like a thundering cataract. Yet day by day the Lord also pours out his steadfast love upon me, and through the night I sing his songs and pray to God who gives me life.

PSALM 42:7-8 TLB

. . . I will pray.

My Lord in Heaven,

My friend is facing some real challenges right now. Years of being wounded emotionally are coming to a head. I've never seen her so down. It's almost like she's given up hope that anything positive can happen to her. And whenever anything remotely negative happens, she takes it as another sign that she's doomed to a life of unhappiness.

I know You value her so highly, Lord—yet I'm not sure how to communicate that to her. When she looks at the future, she sees only bleak prospects. But I know that when You envision her future, You've got great plans in store for her. And I know You want to heal her of the emotional wounds she's suffered all these years—all those voices that haunt her and make her doubt herself.

Lord, thank You that You have wonderful things ahead for my friend. Please give me the right words to say, to encourage her that her past doesn't have to define who she is now. And help her to see that You've got more planned for her than she's ever dared to dream.

Amen.

Apt words have power to assuage
The tumors of a troubled mind
And are as balm to fester'd wounds.
John Milton

When my friend or family member needs physical healing . . .

He himself bore our sins in his body on the tree,
that we might die to sin and live to righteousness.
By his wounds you have been healed.

1 PETER 2:24 RSV

❖

[The Lord says] For you who honor me, goodness will shine
on you like the sun, with healing in its rays.

MALACHI 4:2 NCV

❖

No doubt you know that God anointed Jesus of Nazareth
with the Holy Spirit and with power. Then Jesus went
around doing good and healing all who were oppressed by the
Devil, for God was with him.

ACTS 10:38 NLT

❖

O LORD my God,
I cried to You for help, and You healed me.

PSALM 30:2 NASB

Dear Lord,

I could hear the fear in my friend's voice when she called. Someone in her family needs healing—and things are looking pretty hopeless. I didn't know quite what to say to reassure her. I felt inadequate and stumbled over my words.

What I do know is that You're a God of healing, Lord. Even so, I don't want to give my friend a bunch of pat answers. That's the easy way out and won't help her. So please help me to respond to her with words of comfort and hope when she tells me about her fears.

Thank You, Lord, that nothing is too hard for You. After all, if You could raise someone from the dead, why couldn't You heal any injury? I know, as my friend turns to You for comfort, that You'll help her deal with this difficult situation. Thank You for Your promise that You'll never leave us—You'll be right by us, no matter what challenge we face. I ask for your healing touch and thank You for taking away our fears, as we release them into Your hands, confident that You're able to do great things.

Amen.

No one ever looks in vain to the Great Physician.

F. F. Bosworth

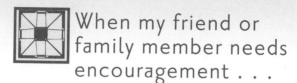 # When my friend or family member needs encouragement . . .

*Let us hold fast to the confession of our hope without
wavering, for he who has promised is faithful.
And let us consider how to provoke one another to love
and good deeds, not neglecting to meet together,
as is the habit of some, but encouraging one another,
and all the more as you see the Day approaching.*
HEBREWS 10:23-25 NRSV

*May the God of steadfastness and encouragement
grant you to live in harmony with one another,
in accordance with Christ Jesus, so that together
you may with one voice glorify the God and Father
of our Lord Jesus Christ.*
ROMANS 15:5-6 NRSV

*Encourage the timid, help the weak,
be patient with everyone.*
1 THESSALONIANS 5:14

. . . I will pray.

Dear Lord,

I've done everything I know to do, said everything I can think of to say. I've tried joking and preaching, even shouting. But nothing I do can break my friend out of the pit of dread and discouragement she has dug for herself. I want to help, but I just don't know what to do anymore. To tell the truth, I was thinking about just walking away. Who needs that kind of downer every day—but then I remembered two things: friends don't leave friends, and You are the greatest encourager of all.

I'm sorry for waiting so long to come to You. I guess I thought I could snap her out of it. In other words, I overestimated myself and underestimated You. Now I pray You will shine Your light on my friend. Open her eyes to see that while we all suffer disappointments at times, there are a lot more happy, uplifting things going on. And nothing that happens to us can compare with the joy and happiness You bring to our lives.

Lord, I've exhausted all my ideas and options. I pray that You would come in and set things right with my friend. Lift her up and let her see her life from Your perspective. Encourage her in Your own special way.

Amen.

Encouragement is oxygen to the soul.

George M. Adams

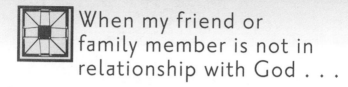

When my friend or family member is not in relationship with God . . .

[The Lord said] I have loved you with an everlasting love;
Therefore with lovingkindness I have drawn you.
JEREMIAH 31:3 NKJV

❖

I will give them an heart to know me, that I am the LORD:
and they shall be my people, and I will be their God.
JEREMIAH 24:7 KJV

❖

"People will no longer have to teach their neighbors and
relatives to know the LORD, because all people will know me,
from the least to the most important," says the LORD.
JEREMIAH 31:34 NCV

❖

[The Lord God says] The nations will know me when they
see me prove how holy I am in what I do through you.
EZEKIEL 38:16 NCV

. . . I will pray.

Lord in Heaven,

I feel so sad that I can't share my life completely with my friend. It would be so great if we could pray together about things, watch You bring the answers, and celebrate Your goodness together. But we don't have that. He says he doesn't believe that prayer makes a difference, maybe because You don't care and maybe because You don't even exist.

I just want to shake him. How can he be so blind about something that seems so obvious to me? How can he live his life without You in it? I just don't understand!

Forgive him, Father. Look beyond his stubborn refusal to see the truth. Give me opportunities to share things that will help him understand how great it is to know You. Even then, though, it won't be enough unless Your Holy Spirit opens his eyes and his heart to see how much You love Him.

Thank You for loving my friend even more than I do. I know You've been waiting a long time to be in a close, loving relationship with him, because You wait for all of us that way. And thank You for the hope that, someday soon, we'll be able to share all the good things You bring into our lives.

Amen.

Our task is to live our personal communion with Christ with such intensity as to make it contagious.

Paul Tournier

When my church needs to be strengthened . . .

How lovely is thy dwelling place,
O LORD of hosts!
My soul longs, yea, faints
for the courts of the LORD;
my heart and flesh sing for joy
to the living God. . . .
Blessed are those who dwell in thy house,
ever singing thy praise!
PSALM 84:1-2, 4 RSV

❖

Let us not give up meeting together, as some are in the habit
of doing, but let us encourage one another—and all the more
as you see the Day approaching.
HEBREWS 10:25

❖

It is good and pleasant
when God's people live together in peace!
PSALM 133:1 NCV

❖

Make me truly happy by agreeing wholeheartedly with each
other, loving one another, and working together
with one heart and purpose.
PHILIPPIANS 2:2 NLT

. . . I will pray.

Dear Lord,

There's been so much murmuring in our church lately. For some reason, people seem divided over lots of different issues. It worries me. I mean, how great a witness can we be when we can't even agree on basic things within our own church walls? What does that say to our community?

I know this isn't Your desire for Your Church, Lord. That You want us to be working together and unified. And if enough of us in the congregation share that desire, I know it will overcome anything else that might be trying to weaken our church.

So help our church come together, Lord. Help us to support our leaders, as they make decisions that affect all of us. Thank You that You can help us put aside our differences and that we can grow even closer together, as a body, and be true witnesses for You. Help us focus on You and Your plans for us, and give us peace and guidance for the future.

Amen.

In her voyage across the ocean of this world, the church is like a great ship being pounded by the waves of life's different stresses. Our duty is not to abandon ship but to keep her on her course.

Saint Boniface

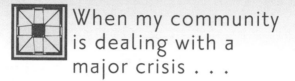

When my community is dealing with a major crisis . . .

He will deliver the needy who cry out, the afflicted who have
no one to help.
PSALM 72:12

❖

I urge, then, first of all, that request, prayers, intercession and
thanksgiving be made for everyone—for kings and all those in
authority, that we may live peaceful and quiet lives in all
godliness and holiness.
1 TIMOTHY 2:1–2

❖

God is our protection and our strength. He always helps in
times of trouble.
PSALM 46:1 NCV

❖

Let us therefore come boldly to the throne of grace, that we
may obtain mercy and find grace to help in time of need.
HEBREWS 4:16 NKJV

. . . I will pray.

Dear Lord,

Our community has never faced a crisis like this before—at least not that I can remember. So many people are hurting and wondering what they will do next. Some have lost everything, even members of their family.

I know that You are here with us, helping us pick up the pieces and start over. I can feel You here even in the middle of all this devastation. Thank You for proving once again that You are willing to face every crisis right along with us. Nothing can make You abandon us in our time of need. It's just like You promised in the Bible, "You will never leave us or forsake us."

Lord, I pray for our community leaders. They must feel so overwhelmed right now. Give them wisdom and strengthen them for the days ahead. And help each one of us to do what we can to make things easier for our neighbors and friends, to share what we have and show kindness and thoughtfulness. Give hope to those who are feeling hopeless and joy to those who are suddenly so sad. Later, Lord, help us remember the lessons this crisis has taught us about trusting in You.

Amen.

The longer I live, the more convincing proofs I see of this truth—God governs in the affairs of men.

Benjamin Franklin

When I see injustice in the world around me . . .

Speak up for those who cannot speak for themselves,
for the rights of all who are destitute.
Speak up and judge fairly;
defend the rights of the poor and needy.
PROVERBS 31:8-9

❖

He has told you, O man, what is good;
And what does the LORD require of you
But to do justice, to love kindness,
And to walk humbly with your God?
MICAH 6:8 NASB

❖

The word of the LORD is upright;
and all his work is done in faithfulness.
He loves righteousness and justice;
the earth is full of the steadfast love of the LORD.
PSALM 33:4-5 RSV

❖

Blessed (Happy, fortunate, to be envied) is he who
considers the weak and the poor; the Lord will deliver him
in the time of evil and trouble.
PSALM 41:1 AMP

. . . I will pray.

Lord of All,

Sometimes I wonder if there's such a thing as real justice in this world. It seems like every time I watch the news, another criminal is getting away with murder—literally! Those who can afford the best lawyers seem to look a little more innocent than those who can't. It makes me angry and frankly, a little scared to see things getting so out of balance.

I know You care about the injustices of the world, too, Lord, that it breaks Your heart when the guilty go free and the innocent end up being punished. But I also know that You've promised that one day, You will judge everyone fairly. Those who didn't find justice here on earth will receive it in heaven.

So, until then, help me to pray for those who are the true victims—that they would know Your peace. And thank You that You do have things in control and that You are a fair and loving God, able to judge the true motives of men's hearts.

Amen.

Man's capacity for justice makes democracy possible;
but man's inclination to injustice
makes democracy necessary.

Reinhold Niebuhr

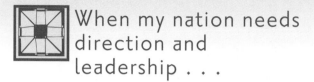# When my nation needs direction and leadership . . .

[The Lord said] If my people who are called by my name humble themselves, and pray and seek my face, and turn from their wicked ways, then I will hear from heaven, and will forgive their sin and heal their land.
2 CHRONICLES 7:14 RSV

❖

Blessed is the nation whose God is the LORD.
PSALM 33:12 KJV

❖

I help kings to govern and rulers to make fair laws.
PROVERBS 8:15 NCV

❖

When a country is lawless, it has one ruler after another; but when it is led by a man with understanding and knowledge, it continues strong.
PROVERBS 28:2 NCV

❖

Loyalty and truth keep a king in power; he continues to rule if he is loyal.
PROVERBS 20:28 NCV

. . . I will pray.

Heavenly Father,

"One nation, under God, indivisible"—is that really our nation's motto? It seems we've strayed so far from that pledge. It seems like people are always pointing fingers, blaming others when things go wrong. And our leaders—sometimes it looks like they care more about keeping their jobs than keeping our country on track. Then there's all that red state/blue state business.

Lord, I know You are the only one who can help us get our nation back on track. Instead of finding fault with each other, we need to work together to find answers—no matter what political party we support. Please help our leaders make right choices so that our country has godly direction for the future. Help us, as a nation, not to be so critical of our leaders, but to recognize their sacrifices and work alongside them.

Thank You that as we pray for our leaders and support them, they'll have Your wisdom to make good choices—and our country can truly be united once again.

Amen.

If we are to be "One Nation Under God,"
we can only do so when we unite and commit to
continue in prayer.

From "Prayer Lines," the official newsletter of
the National Day of Prayer

When I encounter the needy . . .

Blessed are those who help the poor.
PROVERBS 14:21 NLT

❖

If you help the poor, you are lending to the LORD
—and he will repay you!
PROVERBS 19:17 NLT

❖

Whoever gives to the poor will lack nothing.
PROVERBS 28:27 NRSV

❖

There will always be poor people in the land. Therefore I
command you to be openhanded toward your brothers and
toward the poor and needy in your land.
DEUTERONOMY 15:11

❖

If a brother or sister is naked and lacks daily food, and one of
you says to them, "Go in peace; keep warm and eat your fill,"
and yet you do not supply their bodily needs, what is the good
of that? So faith by itself, if it has no works, is dead.
JAMES 2:15-17 NRSV

. . . I will pray.

Dear Lord,

Sometimes I feel overwhelmed by the needs around me. When we're riding in the car, I look out and see a homeless person at the corner begging for change. When I turn on the TV, there's another commercial about the starving kids in Africa, their eyes hollow, their stomachs big and bloated. How can I help these people? I feel like my little bit of change won't do much for them. It might help temporarily, but what about tomorrow?

Lord, I know You have a heart for the needy—that Your own heart aches when You see people hurting. And I know it pleases You when I feel that same compassion for others—when I stop and listen to someone who's hurting and needs to talk or when I give generously as the offering plate is passed to help a family in crisis.

Thank You, Lord, for the loving-kindness you pour out on all people. You know the heart-cry of every person, and You are always waiting to help all those who ask. You are a good and faithful God.

Amen.

What does love look like? It has hands to help others. It has feet to hasten to the poor and needy. It has eyes to see misery and want. It has ears to hear the sighs and sorrows of men. That is what love looks like.

Saint Augustine of Hippo